75 Quick and Easy Solutions to Common Classroom Disruptions

Bryan Harris
Cassandra Goldberg

GOVERNORS STATE UNIVERSITY
UNIVERSITY PARK, IL

EYE ON EDUCATION
6 DEPOT WAY WEST, SUITE 106
LARCHMONT, NY 10538
(914) 833–0551
(914) 833–0761 fax
www.eyeoneducation.com

A sincere effort was made to supply the identity of those who created specific strategies. Any omissions were unintentional.

Library of Congress Cataloging-in-Publication Data

Harris, Bryan.
  75 quick and easy solutions to common classroom disruptions / Bryan Harris, Cassandra Goldberg.
    p. cm.
  ISBN 978-1-59667-209-3
1. Classroom management. 2. School discipline. 3. Behavior modification. I. Goldberg, Cassandra.
II. Title. III. Title: Seventy-five quick and easy solutions to common classroom disruptions.
  LB3011.H275 2011
  371.102'4--dc23   2011043018

Sponsoring Editor: Robert Sickles
Production Editor: Lauren Davis
Copyeditor: Lesli J. Favor
Designer and Compositor: Rick Soldin
Cover Designer: Dave Strauss, 3FoldDesign
Cover Image: EDHAR/Shutterstock

Also Available from Eye On Education

Battling Boredom:
99 Strategies to Spark Student Engagement
Bryan Harris

50 Ways to Improve Student Behavior:
Simple Solutions to Complex Challenges
Annette Breaux and Todd Whitaker

What Do You Say When...?
Best Practice Language for Improving Student Behavior
Hal Holloman and Peggy H. Yates

What Great Teachers Do Differently:
17 Things That Matter Most (2nd Edition)
Todd Whitaker

How the Best Teachers Avoid
the 20 Most Common Teaching Mistakes
Elizabeth Breaux

Reducing the Risk, Increasing the Promise:
Strategies for Student Success
Sherrel Bergmann and Judith Allen Brough

Helping Students Motivate Themselves:
Practical Answers to Classroom Challenges
Larry Ferlazzo

Solving Behavior Problems in Math Class:
Academic, Learning, Social, and Emotional Empowerment
Jennifer Taylor-Cox

101 "Answers" for New Teachers and their Mentors:
Effective Teaching Tips for Daily Classroom Use (2nd Edition)
Annette L. Breaux

'Tween Crayons and Curfews:
Tips for Middle School Teachers
Heather Wolpert-Gawron

The Passion-Driven Classroom:
A Framework for Teaching and Learning
Angela Maiers and Amy Sandvold

Dropout Prevention Fieldbook:
Best Practices from the Field
Franklin P. Schargel

Contents

Acknowledgments

My deepest appreciation first and foremost goes to those classroom teachers, administrators, and school leaders who have given me the opportunity to observe their craft. Teachers are the heart and soul of our society, and I count it a privilege to work with them and help them on their journey. Teaching is hard work, and we all owe a debt of gratitude to those talented, committed, and gifted educators who guide and nurture our children.

I count myself among the most blessed people on the planet. I have tremendous support from my family, colleagues, and the greater education community.

My wife, Becky, and my sons, Andrew and Jeremy, continue to be my heart, and I *still* count it as a privilege to go home to them every day.

My colleagues and friends in the Casa Grande Elementary School District are supportive beyond belief. Dr. Frank Davidson's consistent, patient, and clear leadership has made us all better.

Bob Sickles, Elaine Vislocky, Lauren Davis, Jon Rothman, and the entire team at Eye On Education have been a great support. Their encouragement, feedback, and guidance have made this project better.

A special thank you goes to Eric Jensen—author, friend, and leader in the brain-based learning movement—for his continued support, guidance, and mentorship.

Cassie Goldberg has been a wonderful partner on this project. Her ideas, insights, and perspective have made this book better.

—Bryan

For their endless support throughout my life and this adventure, my sincerest gratitude is extended to the following people.

My husband, Raymond, whose witty sense of humor gets me through the toughest of days and whose laughter makes the best of days that much more enjoyable.

My mom, Sue, my dad, Chuck, and my sisters, Danni, Jess, and Erin, who have helped me walk when my legs were "broken" and encouraged me to follow my dreams. Their support reminds me daily why I am so lucky to have them in my life.

Bob Sickles, Lauren Davis, and their team at Eye On Education for their continued support of Bryan's work and for letting me come along and enjoy the ride.

And last, Dr. Maria Berecin-Rascon and Bryan Harris for giving me the amazing opportunity to work for Casa Grande Elementary School District as a special education teacher and instructional specialist. Their continued leadership, support, and enthusiasm for this profession are greatly admired and appreciated.

—Cassie

About the Authors

Bryan Harris is Director of Professional Development and Public Relations for the Casa Grande Elementary School District in Casa Grande, Arizona. As a former teacher and elementary school principal, he understands that teaching and managing students is both challenging and rewarding. He has a passion for helping teachers find creative, dynamic, and effective ways to engage and manage students. His dynamic and practical presentations make him a sought-after speaker and consultant. He has presented to thousands of educators across the country on the topics of student engagement, classroom management, motivation, and brain-based learning. His first book, *Battling Boredom* (Eye On Education, 2010), is considered one of the best resources available on the topic of student engagement. He can be reached through his Web site, www.bryan-harris.com.

Cassandra Goldberg is Special Education Instructional Specialist for the Casa Grande Elementary School District in Casa Grande, Arizona. She received her bachelor's degree from SUNY Oneonta in Human Ecology with a concentration in Child Development and Child and Family Studies in Oneonta, New York, and a master's degree in Elementary and Special Education from Roberts Wesleyan College in Rochester, New York. She has experience working with students and educators from preschool through middle school providing support, guidance, and staff development in the areas of instructional planning, classroom management, differentiated instruction, and technology-based data collection.

Introduction

Teachers have two great dreams—to work with students who try to learn,
and to escape from the constant struggle against misbehavior.

—C. M. Charles, *The Synergetic Classroom*

I've tried everything I can think of and nothing seems to work for this child. Taking away privileges seems to have no impact. I've called home; that didn't work. Visits to the principal's office don't seem to work either. I've even tried giving the child something to work toward, such as a reward, but that only changed the behavior for a few days. After a while everything went back to the way it was before. In some ways the behavior even got worse. It wouldn't be so bad if it weren't for the impact the child's behavior has on all the other students in class. I've tried a bunch of interventions, but nothing seems to work!

If you are a teacher, administrator, academic coach, or parent who has worked with a challenging student, you know all too well the frustration of trying intervention after intervention only to see little or no improvement in behavior. "I've tried that; it didn't work" is a response we often hear from teachers who are on the front lines trying to help students improve their behavior.

We wrote this book because teaching is hard work. It's even harder when teachers have to deal with misbehaving, off-task, and sometimes disrespectful students. While the vast majority of students in our classrooms are compliant, respectful, and a joy to teach, those few students who exhibit difficult behaviors can wreak havoc on a classroom environment. Out of necessity, teachers often have to spend significant time and effort helping these challenging students develop the skills, attitudes, and positive behaviors that will help them to be successful. It can be a challenge to find the time to assist these students while still teaching the core content curriculum.

In our work in classrooms, we have seen a pattern with the *types* of behaviors teachers most often have to address with students. Teachers commonly deal with students who

- **blurt out** answers, comments, or questions during whole-group instruction, at inappropriate times, or in an inappropriate tone of voice. These students can severely disrupt the flow, energy, and concentration of other students. Often these students are engaged in the content of the lesson and are eager to share, but sometimes they blurt out as a result of a desire to push the teacher's buttons or disrupt class. Regardless, these students need to learn how to control their thoughts, actions, and voices.

- **side talk** during whole-group, small-group, or solo activities. Much like the students who blurt out, these students often are energized, engaged, and want to talk about the lesson. At other times these students want to connect with their friends or outright avoid work. These students need to learn when it is appropriate to talk and when it isn't.

- exhibit **rude or disrespectful** behavior toward the teacher or toward their peers. Most commonly this behavior is overt and obvious to everyone in the class. These students may use inappropriate language, have negative body language, or demonstrate bullying-type behaviors toward other students. These students need to learn how to get their needs met in positive and appropriate ways.

- **zone out or lack focus** during critical learning times. These students may or may not be labeled ADHD, but they seem to lack the ability to stay focused. Though these students are not always causing overt discipline problems, the challenge of motivating them can be overwhelming. Often these students will do just fine in the immediate presence of the teacher, but once the teacher leaves their side, they zone out once again. These students need to learn how to monitor their own learning and to stay focused.

- **don't try or give up easily** when given a classroom task or assignment. Much like the students who zone out, these students are not always difficult in the sense that they distract other students. However, it can be a challenge for teachers to convince them to buy into the work and put forth effort. Some of these students have well-developed coping skills, and they have learned that if they refuse, stall, or mimic, they will get out of work altogether. These students need to experience success and get feedback in order to motivate themselves to tackle classroom tasks.

Specific, practical, and easy-to-use interventions for these five common classroom disruptions are the focus of this book. Unlike other books that provide a general listing of classroom management strategies, we've chosen to align interventions to these five common disruptive behaviors. These interventions focus on helping students to build the skills they need in order to be successful in the classroom.

Why Do Students Misbehave?

Effective teachers know that in order to truly help a student change an inappropriate behavior, they have to get to the root causes and consider the core of the problem (Waller, 2008). When confronted with an inappropriate student behavior, the most effective teachers ask themselves one question: How can I help prevent this from happening again? Teachers should consider not only the most effective immediate consequence but also what interventions will help prevent future occurrences. Part of the process of assisting children in developing necessary skills is getting to the root of why they behave as they do. So, this all begs the question: Why do some students misbehave? Below is a partial list of reasons students may misbehave (Kottler, 2008):

- They are probing boundaries.

- They are mimicking the actions of others.

- They have a strong curiosity about something.

- They desire attention.

- They desire power.

- They are bored or frustrated.

- They have an emotional reaction to something that happened outside of the classroom.

75 Quick and Easy Solutions to Common Classroom Disruptions

- They feel their dignity is threatened.

- They have difficulty handling disagreements.

- They have egocentric personalities.

- They lack self-control (they are impulsive).

- There are unclear directions or expectations.

- They lack basic academic or cognitive skills.

- They have a low tolerance for frustration.

- Home or peer pressure reinforces the behavior.

- They have underlying emotional, physical, psychological, or learning disorders.

And let's not forget that sometimes it is just plain fun to misbehave a little. As you work with students who break rules, misbehave, or disrupt class, it is important to spend time thinking about why they misbehave. When considering appropriate classroom interventions, *why* a student does something is every bit as important as *what* he or she is doing. It is critical to understand the causes of the misbehavior so that you can use the appropriate intervention. When you don't consider the question of why, it is possible that the intervention could actually make the behavior worse.

Dealing with Challenging Behaviors

It is important to remember that, in many cases, the students who are challenging in the classroom are the ones who have problems of their own outside the classroom. When dealing with challenging behaviors, effective teachers first and foremost think about how they can provide the student with structures, interventions, and supports so that the student learns skills to improve in the future. We know that punishment alone rarely teaches a child the skills necessary to act appropriately in the future (Tileston, 2004). The effective teacher isn't first concerned with punishment but rather considers how to provide the structure so that the behavior doesn't happen again.

To work effectively with challenging students, teachers need to have a plan to address misbehaviors when they occur. In the majority of classrooms, it is not a matter of *if* some students will misbehave but *when*. Therefore, teachers should have a plan that consists of specific interventions for when those times arise. Before implementing specific interventions for the five common classroom disruptions, teachers should consider some simple, yet profound assumptions. When working with challenging students, it is important to remember these key ideas:

- **All behavior happens for a reason.** Although children may not be able to clearly express what is going on in their minds, there is usually some sort of payoff for a negative behavior. In order to help students grow, teachers must help students become aware of the problem; they also need to make students full partners in the process of finding a solution. Students who have interventions and strategies *done to* them often rebel because they have no voice in the process. Teachers shouldn't see correcting inappropriate behavior solely as a teacher responsibility. The frustration of "I've tried that; it didn't work" often results from the teacher trying dozens of interventions without including the child in the process.

- **Avoid becoming defensive about a child's behavior.** Rarely does a student plot to make the teacher's life miserable. He or she usually doesn't enter the classroom with a plan to cause chaos or to disrupt the lesson. More often than not, the student is trying to get his or her needs met, albeit in inappropriate ways. Although it is natural to be irritated or concerned by a student's behavior, once the teacher or adult takes the behavior as a personal attack, he or she becomes part of the problem. Keep your cool, remain the adult, and don't take the child's behavior personally.

- **Change the mindset.** If children came to us as they *should* be, there would be no reason to have teachers in the first place. As teachers, we learn a great deal from our most challenging students. For some, finding solutions may take a different way of thinking about difficult students; they need caring and patient adults to teach them social and behavioral skills as much as they need teachers to help them master content knowledge. The students with the most challenging behaviors need the very best teachers.

- **Maintain student dignity.** For some students, it is more honorable to act bad than appear stupid. Maintaining student dignity involves valuing the child and addressing his or her behavior without making judgments about character, background, or personality. Many traditional discipline methods such as name on the board, sarcasm, intimidation, and threats directly attack a student's dignity.

Before Implementing the Interventions

All students, whether they exhibit positive or negative behaviors, will thrive in a classroom environment in which the teacher has the basics of good classroom management in place. The teacher must establish the foundations of a positive classroom environment before utilizing the specific interventions for the five common disruptions. The interventions in this book do not replace whole-group rules, procedures, and processes. Rather, the interventions outlined here are designed to enhance a good classroom management plan. Without the basics of an effective, comprehensive plan in place in a classroom, the specific interventions may not live up to their potential to help students. When developing a classroom management plan, remember that all students need the following:

- positive, clear, and consistently enforced rules and procedures

- explicit, clear directions for activities, participation, and outcomes

- a quality, challenging curriculum that meets their instructional needs

- positive, frequent, and timely feedback about their progress toward meeting instructional goals

- well-planned, engaging, and interactive lessons and activities that are relevant to their lives

- a caring, patient, and respectful teacher who is committed to helping students develop social and emotional skills as well as content knowledge

5-Step Plan for Dealing with Difficult Student Behavior

When dealing with any challenging student behavior, whether the ones listed here or others, it is helpful to have a process to work through as you implement the interventions. The following 5-Step Plan will assist you as you engage students with specific interventions.

Step 1. Label the problem behavior.

- The student has a problem with . . .

Step 2. Describe the problem behavior.

- Who is involved?

- What kinds of behaviors are exhibited?

- When does the problem behavior occur?

- Are there any indicators or signs that the behavior is about to occur?

Step 3. Ask why.

- Ask yourself (the teacher, parent, adult) why this behavior might be happening.

- If appropriate, ask the student to explain his or her ideas or thoughts about the behavior and the solution.

Step 4. Brainstorm specific interventions.

- Utilize peers and print resources for additional ideas.

- Narrow the interventions to between three and five. Refer to steps 2 and 3 when considering interventions.

- Don't duplicate or continue use of previously used interventions that have been unsuccessful.

Step 5. Implement specific interventions.

- Create a timeline for implementation.

- Communicate with parents, the student, the school administration, and any adult who may be impacted by the intervention(s).

- Reflect on a weekly basis and adjust as needed.

- Provide specific feedback to the student throughout the process.

How to Use This Book

As a result of our work with classroom teachers, we have aligned the interventions in this book specifically to the five most common classroom disruptions: *students who blurt out in whole group, students who side talk, students who are rude or disrespectful, students who zone out or lack focus,* and *students who don't try or give up easily.* The descriptions of the interventions that follow in this book have each of the 5 common behaviors listed at the top of the page. The behavior(s) aligned to that specific intervention is highlighted with a white border. Although we have chosen to align specific interventions to these common behaviors, with adjustments or modifications the ideas listed here can be used to address other behaviors as well. This is particularly true when a student exhibits behavior in more than one area. After all, it is common for the student who blurts out comments to also side talk at inappropriate times. Therefore, view these interventions as a menu of ideas rather than a checklist of requirements. Some students will respond very well to certain interventions and not so well to others. When working with students, it is essential to have numerous, effective interventions prepared and ready to go. This book is designed to be a resource of ideas to refer to often as you work to find the right interventions for your students. The following Intervention Matrix serves as a reference to help you identify effective solutions for common classroom disruptions. There is also an Index of Interventions by Behavior on page 79 that outlines the strategies by the 5 common disruptions.

Intervention Matrix

Intervention	Page #	Blurting Out in Whole Group	Side Talking	Rude/Dis-respectful Behavior	Zoning Out/Lack of Focus	Doesn't Try/Gives Up Easily
A Head Start	1				X	X
Advance Organizers	2				X	X
Apologize	3			X		
Attention Signal	4	X	X	X	X	X
Audio Recording	5	X	X	X		
Be Brief, Be Positive, Be Gone	6			X	X	X
Be the Model	7	X	X			
Bean Bag	8	X			X	X
Behavior Contracts	9			X		X
Behavior Tracking	10	X	X			
Check-In Statements	11				X	X
Checklists	12				X	X

Intervention	Page #	Blurting Out in Whole Group	Side Talking	Rude/Dis-respectful Behavior	Zoning Out/Lack of Focus	Doesn't Try/Gives Up Easily
Choice of Order	13			X	X	
Chunk Tasks	14				X	X
Clear Directions	15	X	X	X	X	X
Closed Fist	16					X
Color Codes	17				X	
Communicate with Home	18	X	X	X	X	X
Compliments and Congratulations	19	X	X	X	X	X
Concrete Reminders	20	X	X			
Course Evaluation	21			X		X
Describe the Request	22	X	X	X	X	X
Eliminate Distractions	23				X	
Energizers	24	X	X	X	X	X
Engaging Frames	25				X	X
Extend an Invitation	26			X	X	X
Eye Contact	27	X	X	X		
5-Minute Focus Group	28			X	X	X
Focus on Process	29					X
Give a Gift	30			X		X
Give a Job	31			X		
Graph the Results	32	X	X	X	X	X
Greet and Read	33	X	X	X	X	X
Headphones	34		X		X	
Humor	35	X	X	X	X	X

Intervention	Page #	Blurting Out in Whole Group	Side Talking	Rude/Dis-respectful Behavior	Zoning Out/Lack of Focus	Doesn't Try/Gives Up Easily
I Messages	36	X	X	X		
If-Then Statements	37	X	X	X		
Increase Feedback	38	X	X	X	X	X
Learn to Ignore	39	X	X	X		
Likely Before Unlikely	40	X	X	X	X	X
Looks Like, Sounds Like, Feels Like	41	X	X	X	X	X
Minimize Anxiety	42			X		X
Offer the Door	43			X		
Personal Goals	44			X		X
Photographic Evidence	45	X	X			
Planted Questions	46				X	X
Positive Self-Talk	47			X		X
Private Office	48		X		X	
Proximity	49	X	X		X	X
Questions of Concern	50	X	X	X	X	X
Ramp Up Relevance	51			X	X	X
Rating Scales	52	X	X	X	X	X
Right to Pass	53			X		X
Secret Signal	54	X	X			
Sentence Starters	55				X	X
SLANT	56	X	X	X	X	X
Smile	57	X	X	X	X	X
Solicit Good Intentions	58	X	X	X		
Special Seating	59				X	

Intervention	Page #	Blurting Out in Whole Group	Side Talking	Rude/Dis-respectful Behavior	Zoning Out/Lack of Focus	Doesn't Try/Gives Up Easily
Specific Time Frames	60	X	X	X	X	X
Sponge Activities	61	X	X	X		
Stand and Stretch	62				X	X
Start Statements	63	X	X	X	X	X
Start Strong, End Strong	64	X	X	X		
Stories	65					X
Talking Chips	66	X	X			
Teacher-Approved Toys	67			X	X	
Teaching Spot	68				X	
Thanks in Advance	69	X	X	X		
Three More Minutes, and…	70			X	X	X
Track the Lesson	71			X	X	X
Traffic Light	72				X	X
2 x 10 Method	73			X		
Victory List	74	X	X	X	X	X
What You Could Have Said Was	75	X	X	X		

Interventions

Overview

Just as a car sometimes needs a jump start to get going, some struggling students need a little boost in the form of **A Head Start** on projects, tasks, or assignments. This intervention provides students with a boost in the form of suggestions, ideas, or answers that encourage them to start and complete an assignment.

Putting It All Together

We all like to get something for free. We all like the feeling of getting just a little bit more than what we paid for. Who hasn't been drawn into one of those buy one, get one free sales? Before beginning an assignment, privately talk with the student, explaining that you have made some adjustments to the task that will impact what he or she needs to complete. Explain that you have provided the answers for the first several problems that need to be completed. For example, the teacher may say, "I've done something special for you with this assignment. You can see that there are twenty problems to complete, but I've provided you with the answers to the first three. With only seventeen left, you should be able to complete those easily by the end of the class." This intervention taps into the concept of self-interest to encourage students to begin and stay on track with an assignment or task.

Tips and Variations

- Some teachers object to the appearance of unfairness with this intervention. However, many challenging students are unlikely to complete the assignment at all. This intervention increases the likelihood that the assignment will be completed.

- In addition to providing direct answers, suggest which problems or tasks are easiest, are most difficult, or will take the most time. Giving extra time to complete the assignment or giving **Choice of Order** will also tap into the concept of self-interest.

- This intervention works well with **Be Brief, Be Positive, Be Gone; Chunk Tasks**; and **Engaging Frames**.

ADVANCE ORGANIZERS

Blurting Out in Whole Group | Side Talking | Rude/ Disrespectful Behavior | **Zoning Out/ Lack of Focus** | **Doesn't Try/ Gives Up Easily**

Overview

Advance Organizers provide students with information, context, clues, or a heads-up about upcoming events, activities, or tasks before they take place in the classroom.

Putting It All Together

Although all students benefit from advanced warnings about upcoming events, this intervention is particularly effective for students who tend to get lost during fast-paced lessons or activities or when there is an unexpected change in the schedule. It can be used to signal changes from a normal routine, as a notice of upcoming transitions, or as a way to let students know that they will be expected to move, demonstrate knowledge, or interact with one another. **Advance Organizers** can be given verbally, written on the board or a poster, or given to individual students in the form of a card or Post-It Note. This intervention provides students with the mental framework to consider changes, expectations, and adjustments to their thinking or expectations. The teacher may say, "Jeremy, as a heads-up, I wanted you to know that we'll be doing some partner activities in about 10 minutes. So prepare yourself and start to think about what you could say about the story we just read."

Tips and Variations

- Teachers regularly provide advance warnings to students when they know they will be absent. For example, many teachers say something like "Students, tomorrow I will be absent, and Mrs. Miller will be your substitute teacher. She may not know our full routine, so you will need to be on your best behavior if anything changes or gets moved around."

- **Advance Organizers** differ from graphic organizers in a number of ways. A graphic organizer offers students a method to visually organize information, data, or content. An **Advance Organizer** is a tool or method, similar to a hook, anticipatory set, or introduction, that offers students information in advance of an event.

APOLOGIZE

| Blurting Out in Whole Group | Side Talking | **Rude/ Disrespectful Behavior** | Zoning Out/ Lack of Focus | Doesn't Try/ Gives Up Easily |

Overview

Some children struggle to apologize for their actions because they do not know how to appropriately and properly express remorse or regret. The ability to emotionally account for one's actions is a learned skill that must be overtly taught and modeled.

Putting It All Together

A sincere apology is one way to restore a broken relationship. When the student is calm and in the proper mindset to reflect, have a private conversation in which you prompt the student to consider his or her actions, what caused the inappropriate behavior, and what he or she could do to make things better. Explain that the purpose of an apology is twofold: First, it shows the other person that you recognize what happened and that you are sorry. Second, it helps both parties to move past the incident. Students need to know that apologies help them as well. Once they apologize for an action, they are better able to move past the hard feelings or guilt. Although receiving a reduced punishment or consequence should not be the purpose of the apology, students should know that a sincere, heartfelt apology (with a corresponding promise of improved future behavior) often results in a less severe punishment.

Tips and Variations

- Some students need examples of the exact words or phrases to use when attempting an apology. Use **Sentence Starters,** such as "I would like to say I'm sorry for …"

- Many students do not have good models of apologetic behaviors or attitudes. It is important for teachers to model apologies by admitting their errors and asking students to forgive them when they have made a mistake.

- Acknowledge to the student that apologizing is not an easy thing to do. There are typically very strong emotions attached, and it can be difficult to admit wrongdoing.

- Sincerity is the key, so students should not be forced to apologize before they are ready.

Overview

An effective **Attention Signal** is a foundational tool in every classroom. Although all students benefit from an **Attention Signal**, it is a particularly powerful intervention with challenging students.

Putting It All Together

As a technique for gaining and maintaining student attention, an overt signal is a necessity in every classroom. When choosing an **Attention Signal**, consider the maturity, age, and ability level of the students. After you choose a signal, follow these steps in order for the signal to be effective:

- **Explain** to students what the signal is, how it will be used, and what its purpose is.
- **Model** for students the use of the signal, including the student response.
- **Practice** the signal and provide feedback.

Some of the most effective **Attention Signals** require students to respond with a physical action. For example, if the Give Me 5 signal is used (the teacher raises a hand, showing five fingers, and verbally asks students for their attention), the students respond by looking at the teacher and raising their hands also. Other **Attention Signals** include chimes, bells, rain sticks, claps or clapping patterns, and train whistles.

Tips and Variations

- Generally it is not a good idea to flick the lights as a signal. This action typically excites and energizes students and often results in students blurting out inappropriate comments.
- Have backup **Attention Signals** prepared because sometimes a signal loses its effectiveness after the novelty has worn off. When you introduce a new one, it is important to explain, model, and practice the new signal.
- To increase the effectiveness of the **Attention Signal**, combine with **Engaging Frames**, **Rating Scales**, or **Specific Time Frames**.
- Before expecting student attention, consider what they are currently involved in and how much time they need to stop and refocus.

AUDIO RECORDING

| Blurting Out in Whole Group | Side Talking | Rude/ Disrespectful Behavior | Zoning Out/ Lack of Focus | Doesn't Try/ Gives Up Easily |

Overview

Listening to oneself on an **Audio Recording** can provide a unique and novel opportunity for a student to reflect on behavior. A recording of classroom interactions provides both the student and the teacher the opportunity to reflect, question, and consider the impact of behavior on others in the classroom.

Putting It All Together

This intervention should be used carefully and only after the school administration, parents, and students are made aware of the process and procedures that you will use. Let the students know that you will be recording parts of the lesson or day with the purpose of learning about the class. Students do not always need to be told exactly when the recording will begin or end or that the focus will be solely on them. The purpose of recording the class is to gather information and feedback about student focus, the pace of the lesson, the appropriateness of the learning tasks, and the overall classroom climate. Once the class has been recorded, the information can be used in several ways. First, the teacher should listen to the recording alone in order to reflect on clarity of directions, pacing of lessons, and the focus of the students. Then it may be appropriate to meet with individual students to listen to portions of the recording. In private discussions with students, point out things like "Raymond, did you notice that when I was giving directions for our group project, you interrupted three times?" Use the information collected from the recording to lead a discussion about how individual behavior impacts the class.

Tips and Variations

- Do not play the recording for the whole class unless it is to point out positive group behavior and to congratulate students on their accomplishments or growth.

- Audio recording equipment is easier to set up than a video camera, and students often forget they are being recorded because there is no video camera to "catch" their behavior. In addition, some students may feel the need to "play" or show off for the video camera.

Overview

When used correctly, this intervention combines the power of **Proximity** with concentrated feedback and physical space to help a student refocus on a task or assignment.

Putting It All Together

Some students struggle with multipart or layered directions and are more likely to experience success and compliance when directions are clear, to the point, and brief. Therefore, when you provide directions, give feedback regarding behavior, or correct behavior, the statements should **Be Brief**. Statements, directions, and feedback should also **Be Positive** and declared using a tone that demonstrates that the teacher believes that the child can and will comply and participate. Because many challenging students expect to hear negative comments about their behavior or character, a positive tone of voice and supportive nonverbal communication is a must. Therefore, expectations, comments, and feedback should be stated with positive intent. After giving a direction, a task, or setting an expectation—**Be Gone**. That is, literally provide students with the physical space to accomplish tasks without hovering over them. Some students, as long as they are being watched, will play the You Can't Make Me game. It's almost as if they are saying, "Back off and give me some space, and then maybe I'll do it."

Tips and Variations

- As a way to increase feedback about a behavior, combine this intervention with **Check-In Statements, Graph the Results,** or **Rating Scales**.

- Teachers should work to ensure that their verbal and nonverbal communication is congruent. If positive words are used with a negative, doubtful tone or aggressive body language, the power of this strategy is reduced.

- When providing guidance and feedback to challenging students, it is important to remember that many students are very concerned with how they appear to their peers. This is particularly true if a child is stressed, upset, or overwhelmed. During those times, it can be difficult for a child to think clearly or rationally.

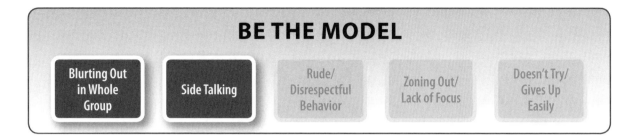

Overview

Modeling expected behavior is at the root of effective teaching and learning. This intervention asks students to **Be the Model** in order to demonstrate the correct and acceptable way to complete tasks or participate in classroom activities.

Putting It All Together

This intervention is best utilized when it has been prearranged with a specific student. In a one-on-one setting, explain to the student that you will be demonstrating to the class the proper procedures and expectations for an activity and that you'd like the student to model for the class the proper way to participate. Provide clear explanations of what you'd like the student to do during the demonstration. If needed, review with the student what to do if students have questions or if things do not go as planned. For example, a student who tends to dominate small-group discussions may be asked to model the proper way to use **Talking Chips** in a small-group discussion. That same student could also be asked to share reasons why taking turns and following procedures is important.

Tips and Variations

- In order for this intervention to be effective, the teacher needs to consistently and correctly model the expected behaviors as well. For example, if part of the expectations are to use *please* and *thank you* when sharing materials, the teacher needs to use those phrases as well.

- In most cases, it is not recommended to have students model the inappropriate ways to behave. Most students, particularly older ones, already know the basic expectations in school, and bad models could encourage students to make fun of the situation. In addition, this intervention is likely to backfire if attempted with rude or disrespectful students because of the opportunity to mock or make light of the expectations in front of their peers.

BEAN BAG

| Blurting Out in Whole Group | Side Talking | Rude/ Disrespectful Behavior | Zoning Out/ Lack of Focus | Doesn't Try/ Gives Up Easily |

Overview

A physical object such as a toy, stuffed animal, or small **Bean Bag** can be a powerful tool to encourage participation, effort, and turn-taking in the classroom. It can be a type of **Concrete Reminder**; students benefit from having a physical object to manipulate and remind them of the procedures, expectations, and time limits.

Putting It All Together

After explaining the procedures and expectations of an assignment or a task, the teacher tosses the **Bean Bag** to a student and prompts him or her with a question, direction, or statement. The student holding the **Bean Bag** is then given the opportunity to respond. Only the student holding the **Bean Bag** should be talking, modeling, or demonstrating during the specified time. Depending on the activity and the question/discussion prompt, the student could toss the **Bean Bag** back to the teacher or to a fellow classmate to continue or follow up on the discussion. This creates opportunities for students to share information in a structured way and also incorporates physical movement.

Tips and Variations

- Model for students exactly how they are expected to toss the **Bean Bag** to one another. It may be necessary to model the difference between "toss" and "throw."

- If a student is unsure of an answer, allow him or her to consult with a partner, or give the student the **Right to Pass**.

- As a small-group option, have students pass the **Bean Bag** during discussions.

- This is an excellent intervention to use with students who tend to dominate or monopolize discussions because it can limit when and how long students are to talk or share.

Overview

A **Behavior Contract** is a mutually agreed upon written document between the teacher(s), student, and the parent(s) that outlines expected behaviors, positive replacement behaviors, incentives for following the contract, and consequences for not following it.

Putting It All Together

Behavior Contracts help formalize behavioral expectations in the classroom. As written agreements, they can help avoid any confusion regarding rules and expectations. When creating a **Behavior Contract**, focus on one behavior and provide students with a clear explanation of when the problem behavior most often occurs and the impact it is having on the classroom or their individual success. Together, through a collaborative process with the parent and student, the teacher helps brainstorm ways to assist the student to achieve the goals written in the contract. Although some students may need to be prompted with a reward or incentive, the reward does not need to be something tangible or expensive. Often students choose rewards such as extra time on the computer, free time to talk with a friend, or a free homework pass.

Tips and Variations

- **Behavior Contracts** can be effectively used in conjunction with **Graph the Results, Personal Goals, and Victory Lists**.

- **Behavior Contracts** are typically not as successful with students who have impulsive behaviors, such as blurting out or being distracted.

- Part of the power of a contract is the fact that it brings attention and focus to a problem.

- This process will likely be unsuccessful without the buy-in and input from a student and family.

BEHAVIOR TRACKING

Blurting Out in Whole Group | **Side Talking** | Rude/ Disrespectful Behavior | Zoning Out/ Lack of Focus | Doesn't Try/ Gives Up Easily

Overview

Some of our most impulsive students don't have a clear understanding of the depth or frequency of the disruptions they create in the classroom. This intervention provides students with a visible, concrete method to track their own behavior and offers them a chance to reflect on the impact of that behavior on others.

Putting It All Together

In a one-on-one setting, explain to the student that you need his or her help in keeping track of the student's behavior. Specifically, be clear and overt about which behaviors are causing a distraction in the class. Provide the student with a Post-It Note, a 3 x 5 card, or a blank sheet of paper, and demonstrate how to use tally marks to count occurrences. Explain that the student is going to keep track of the number of times he or she blurts out comments or side talks at inappropriate times. The goal is to get an honest reflection of the events in the classroom. If needed, provide the student with a **Secret Signal** that will be used to indicate when he or she should tally an occurrence. At the end of the day or class period, review the tally marks with the student and reflect on the number of occurrences, the time of the occurrences, and the impact on other students.

Tips and Variations

- The power of this intervention is that the data is collected by the student. However, if the student is unable to tally occurrences, data can be collected by the teacher or a paraprofessional and shared with the student.

- Save the tracking sheets to show progress over time or use **Graph the Results** or **Victory Lists**.

- The tracking sheets are also helpful when meeting with parents.

- The student could also track each time he or she wanted to blurt or side talk but was able to refrain.

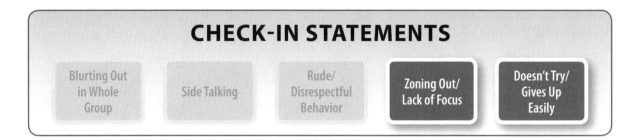

CHECK-IN STATEMENTS

Blurting Out in Whole Group | Side Talking | Rude/ Disrespectful Behavior | **Zoning Out/ Lack of Focus** | **Doesn't Try/ Gives Up Easily**

Overview

A **Check-In Statement** is a personal connection, in the form of a brief verbal statement, that the teacher makes with the purpose of helping a student to focus on tasks and classroom assignments.

Putting It All Together

Typically done during independent work time, **Check-In Statements** provide students with clear directions, information, and statements about the tasks that need to be accomplished as well as a time frame during which they will be held accountable. For example, as the teacher moves about the room to check on student progress, he or she may say, "Andrew, right now we are working on the rough draft of our persuasive essay. Complete the outline of the first paragraph, and I'll be back to check on you in about five minutes. When I come back, please have that section completed. If you finish before five minutes are up, give me a thumbs-up and I'll come to check on you." A statement such as this provides the student with a clear task as well as the time frame during which he or she will be held accountable.

Tips and Variations

- Before making a statement about the task(s) that needs to be completed, ensure that the student has the knowledge and ability to successfully complete those tasks independently.

- If appropriate, ask the student when he or she wants a check-in. For example, "Andrew, how much time do you think it should take to complete the first section of your essay? Great. I'll come back and check on you in about five minutes."

- If too many students have check-in times that are close to one another, it can be easy to lose track of which students need follow-up. This can frustrate both the teacher and the students and provide reluctant or distracted students with an excuse not to work.

CHECKLISTS

Blurting Out in Whole Group

Side Talking

Rude/ Disrespectful Behavior

Zoning Out/ Lack of Focus

Doesn't Try/ Gives Up Easily

Overview

Checklists can serve as a type of road map to help students determine which tasks and assignments need to be accomplished and in what order. Many students are motivated by the ability to track their accomplishments and check off items as they complete them.

Putting It All Together

Provide the student with a blank **Checklist** form and explain that the student will be tracking his or her accomplishments during the day or lesson. Together, the teacher and student review the tasks, assignments, or work that needs to be completed, and the teacher provides a specific time frame for each task. The teacher helps guide the student to list, copy, or brainstorm the tasks that need to be completed in order to meet the expectations of the assignment. As tasks or jobs are completed, the student checks them off the list.

Tips and Variations

- Remember to provide students with time to update their **Checklists** and celebrate their accomplishments. **Checklists** can easily be turned into **Victory Lists** and used to **Communicate with Home**.

- Consider guiding students to place the easiest tasks or jobs at the beginning of the list. This helps build momentum and motivation.

- Some students benefit from the use of multiple **Checklists** for organizing different types of tasks or areas of study. **Color Codes** are an effective way to support the use of multiple **Checklists**.

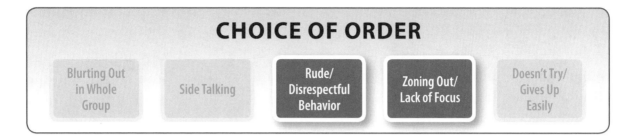

CHOICE OF ORDER

Blurting Out in Whole Group | Side Talking | Rude/ Disrespectful Behavior | Zoning Out/ Lack of Focus | Doesn't Try/ Gives Up Easily

Overview

If teachers view learning as a journey, the route to be taken can and should be different for each student. Allowing some choice in academic tasks is both motivating to students and respectful of individual differences.

Putting It All Together

Choices give students a sense of power and ownership over part of their day and typically result in increased task completion. When students are faced with more than one task or a lengthy assignment, provide them the option of choosing which assignment or which part(s) of the assignment to start with. Although choices are powerful motivators for all students, they are particularly effective with some challenging students when explained in a one-on-one setting. Choices can include the order in which an assignment is completed, the method for demonstrating mastery, the resources used to investigate an answer, the partners they work with to complete a task, or the freedom to move about the classroom to get necessary materials or to seek assistance.

Tips and Variations

● Remember to **Ramp Up Relevance** when providing choices, tasks, and assignments so that students can see a direct connection between their choices and personal relevance. Even when you offer choices, students may not be motivated to complete the tasks if they consider them to be boring, irrelevant, or not at their ability level.

● Utilize student interests to gain insight into how the student might want to demonstrate knowledge. Based on your understanding of the strengths of the student, suggest methods he or she could use to show mastery of content knowledge.

● Some students, particularly those who struggle to focus, may become overwhelmed by too many choices. In those cases, offer the student specific suggestions for the order of tasks, encourage him or her to **Chunk Tasks**, or relate the assignment to a **Personal Goal**.

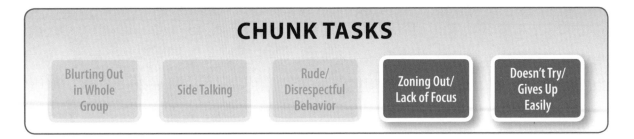

CHUNK TASKS

Blurting Out in Whole Group | Side Talking | Rude/ Disrespectful Behavior | **Zoning Out/ Lack of Focus** | **Doesn't Try/ Gives Up Easily**

Overview

Some students get easily overwhelmed with large assignments or tasks that have multiple steps. Chunking is the process of breaking assignments and activities into smaller, more manageable parts and providing structured directions for each part.

Putting It All Together

Tests, worksheets, projects, and daily activities can easily be broken down into small, manageable tasks. Before giving an assignment to students, let them know that they have options when it comes to completing the requirements of the assignment. For example, they may chunk a thirty-problem worksheet into six sections of five questions, they may fold their paper in half and finish the top questions followed by the ones at the bottom, or they may complete even-numbered questions followed by the odd-numbered questions. When initially teaching students how to break bigger assignments into smaller ones, you will likely need to provide models, examples, and demonstrations of how it should be done. This will include demonstrating what students should do when they get stuck or don't know how to proceed once a certain chunk is completed.

Tips and Variations

● Students' frustration with complex, multipart tasks often increases when they do not see the value, relevance, or reason for participation or effort. In addition to showing students where and how to **Chunk Tasks**, show them how the completion of the tasks is relevant and important to their success.

● Combine **Chunk Tasks** with **Check-In Statements, Choice of Order**, or **Specific Time Frames**.

● Students can chunk assignments by doing any of the following: odds first; evens first; first two, five, or ten problems; last two, five, or ten problems; cut the assignment in half; fold the paper in half; do the easier sections first, etc.

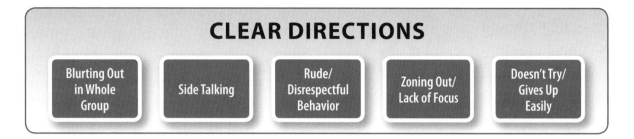

CLEAR DIRECTIONS

| Blurting Out in Whole Group | Side Talking | Rude/ Disrespectful Behavior | Zoning Out/ Lack of Focus | Doesn't Try/ Gives Up Easily |

Overview

Unclear, multipart, and complicated verbal directions often lead to off-task behavior by students. Much of that inappropriate behavior will be reduced when teachers provide **Clear Directions**.

Putting It All Together

Giving effective directions takes time and practice and does not come easily to all teachers. As a result, when working with challenging students, teachers should spend time crafting the words, visuals, and structures that will increase the likelihood that students will follow directions. To give **Clear Directions**, teachers can use the following suggestions:

- Utilize an **Attention Signal** and wait to give directions until all students are ready. Do not talk over students.

- Use the fewest words possible to convey the message.

- Provide a clear time frame that informs students when to begin a task and how much time they have to complete it.

- Give directions immediately before students need to act. Avoid giving directions too far in advance of action because students may forget expectations.

- For projects with multiple parts or steps, provide or suggest a sequence to complete the tasks.

- Anticipate which steps might provide problems or prompt questions from students.

- Provide visual support for directions, such as steps written on the board, icons to represent actions, or checklists.

Tips and Variations

- Avoid statements such as "You're not following directions" or "That's not what I told you to do; you need to follow directions" when students don't follow directions. Rather, consider using **Be Brief, Be Positive, Be Gone**; **Checklists**; or **Proximity**.

- For particularly challenging classes, consider scripting word-for-word the specific directions for tasks. A **5-Minute Focus Group** with a few students could be helpful in determining the best methods for describing actions and directing student behavior.

- Many students benefit from having a brief partner discussion to review steps, to plan for task completion, and to get clarification.

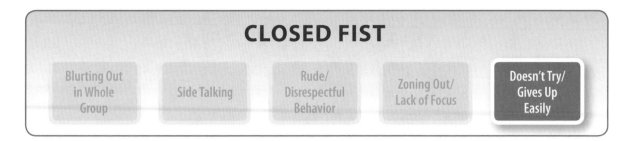

CLOSED FIST

Blurting Out in Whole Group | Side Talking | Rude/ Disrespectful Behavior | Zoning Out/ Lack of Focus | **Doesn't Try/ Gives Up Easily**

Overview

Some students are hesitant to participate in classroom activities for fear of being teased, ridiculed, or called upon when they are unable to answer. This intervention builds confidence in those students and gives them the chance to participate secure in the knowledge that they will only be called upon after they indicate that they'd like to answer a question or provide a comment.

Putting It All Together

Speak with the student privately and explain that you have devised a system that will allow students to indicate when, during a whole-group lesson, they'd like to participate by answering a question or making a comment. This intervention requires that the student raise a hand and indicate his or her confidence on a scale expressed with fingers. When the student raises a hand with a **Closed Fist**, it indicates that he or she does not want to answer the question but is participating by raising a hand just like other students in the class. For some students, this ability to "play along" may be the first step in building confidence. If the student raises a hand and holds up five fingers, it is an expression that he or she has full confidence in the answer and would like to be called upon to participate. Showing one to four fingers can express the level of a student's confidence or willingness to participate. The **Closed Fist** intervention gives students the framework to take the first step to public participation with the understanding that the teacher will respect their wishes.

Tips and Variations

- Monitor the student's progress and participation, but don't be overly concerned if the student stays with a **Closed Fist** for several weeks. Part of the power of this intervention is that it gives power and control to the student. Students also need to know that they can trust the teacher to respect their wishes.

- Consider using **A Head Start** or **Planted Questions** as a way to encourage participation.

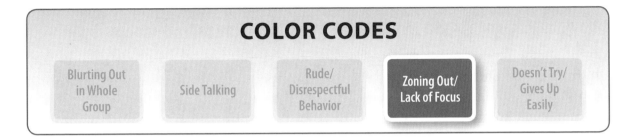

Overview

The use of different colors can provide students with a clear way to organize their learning and can assist in memory, recall, and processing. Color-coded materials also help students when it comes to locating and organizing materials such as folders, handouts, and written work.

Putting It All Together

Some students struggle to remain focused and on task during certain classroom activities such as note-taking or partner work or while organizing materials. The use of **Color Codes** can provide students with directions, reminders, and cues for sorting, organizing, and collecting materials. Provide students with different-colored markers, pens, or highlighters to code and organize their notes in a specific or sequential manner. For example, as students are organizing their materials and notes about the American Revolution, instruct them to highlight *events* in the color green, *personalities* in the color yellow and *facts* in the color blue. This strategy gives students a focus during note-taking and also keys in to their visual memory, which will help them to recall specific information later. **Color Codes** can also help students organize their everyday materials. For example, all students can have red folders for math, blue folders for reading, orange folders for social studies, and so on. This can help students quickly locate materials for a class and help teachers to visually assess if their students have the proper folder for the class.

Tips and Variations

- **Color Codes** are helpful when students are working on long-term, project-oriented tasks. In this case, have students use different-colored codes to organize the process of the tasks, such as items to be completed by a certain date in one color, items that can wait until the end in another, and items that need to be double-checked in another.

- **Color Codes** work well in conjunction with **Checklists** and **Victory Lists.**

COMMUNICATE WITH HOME

| Blurting Out in Whole Group | Side Talking | Rude/ Disrespectful Behavior | Zoning Out/ Lack of Focus | Doesn't Try/ Gives Up Easily |

Overview

For many teachers, the thought of contacting parents brings fear, dread, and anxiety. While it is sometimes the case that challenging students come from difficult families, one of the best tools to help improve behavior is to partner with parents.

Putting It All Together

Teachers can **Communicate with Home** in a variety of ways. Phone calls, e-mails, text messages, handwritten notes, postcards, newsletters, Web sites, and personal conversations are all effective tools that help to connect with families. Teachers should create a plan that outlines specific times and methods that they plan to use to stay in touch with families. When contacting parents regarding a child's inappropriate behavior, always include good news and talk about what you appreciate about the child. All parents like to hear good things about their children. Take the time to listen to parents in order to understand, from their perspective, what can be done to help their child succeed. When anticipating a particularly difficult conversation, consider scripting or outlining talking points before contacting the parent.

Tips and Variations

● It is helpful to remember that parents are sometimes defensive and on guard because the majority of calls or contacts from schools are negative. The only time most parents get a call from school is when their child is hurt or in trouble. Therefore, provide good news, evidence of success, and appreciations as much as possible.

● Combine **Communicate with Home** with **Compliments and Congratulations**, **Graph the Results**, or **Victory List**.

● Offer parents the opportunity to visit the classroom during the day in order to observe what takes place.

● It is helpful to maintain a log of methods, dates, and outcomes of the various attempts you used to **Communicate with Home**.

COMPLIMENTS AND CONGRATULATIONS

| Blurting Out in Whole Group | Side Talking | Rude/ Disrespectful Behavior | Zoning Out/ Lack of Focus | Doesn't Try/ Gives Up Easily |

Overview

Everyone appreciates a genuine compliment and recognition of a job well done. When the teacher takes the time to regularly provide positive statements in the form of **Compliments and Congratulations**, wonderful things can happen in the classroom climate and in the behavior of individual students.

Putting It All Together

A compliment on a personal attribute such as work ethic or congratulations on the achievement of certain goals can be motivating to many children. In addition to a boost in motivation, **Compliments and Congratulations** tell the child that his or her efforts or characteristics are noticed and valued. Some of our students act out in inappropriate ways because they lack a solid, meaningful connection or relationship with the teacher. For some students, it may take additional effort to find positive qualities or behaviors, but the comments do not need to focus solely on achievement or school-related issues. A polite, genuine compliment about a haircut or a new pair of shoes, or congratulations on accomplishing a feat on the athletic field will help to send a message that the student is important beyond what happens in the classroom.

Tips and Variations

● Some students may be sensitive about receiving compliments, praise, or recognition because they aren't used to it, don't know how to receive it, or expect ulterior motives. In those cases, ensure that statements are private, positive, and not followed up with statements about changes in future behavior. Simply give honest compliments and recognition in the moment to send the message that the student is valued and important.

● This intervention can be combined with **Be Brief, Be Positive, Be Gone; Greet and Read; or Rating Scales**, or as a method to **Communicate with Home**.

CONCRETE REMINDERS

Blurting Out in Whole Group | **Side Talking** | Rude/ Disrespectful Behavior | Zoning Out/ Lack of Focus | Doesn't Try/ Gives Up Easily

Overview

Concrete Reminders are real, physical objects that represent an idea, task, expectation, or thought process. Many impulsive students quickly forget verbal reminders or redirections but will respond when a behavioral reminder is offered as a real, concrete object.

Putting It All Together

The power of this intervention is that children are able to touch, manipulate, and use a physical object to remind *themselves* of the expected behavior, thus freeing the teacher from the need for constant verbal redirection. Therefore, the actual physical object does not need to be elaborate or expensive. **Concrete Reminders** can be in the form of common school supplies such as pencils and erasers, simple items such as string, rubber bands, and small, smooth stones, or specially created materials such as cards with pictures or icons printed on them. For example, consider a student who impulsively blurts out comments or answers during a lesson. Privately speak with the student about the need to follow rules and expectations during class and provide him or her with a 3 x 5 card with the phrase "Please raise your hand" written on it. Explain that the card is a physical reminder of the need to raise a hand when he or she wants to participate. Ask the student to hold the card during the whole-group part of the lesson. After the lesson is over, the teacher can either collect the **Concrete Reminder** or ask the student to keep it. It is important to debrief and talk with the student about the effectiveness of the intervention and any adjustments that may need to be made.

Tips and Variations

- Remember to discuss the process with the student and help him or her understand how the object is to be used. Make the process fun and allow the child to provide suggestions.

- Explain that each time the student touches, sees, or uses the **Concrete Reminder**, the student is to repeat the expected behavior in his or her mind.

- **Color Codes** and **Talking Chips** are examples of **Concrete Reminders**.

COURSE EVALUATION

Blurting Out in Whole Group | Side Talking | **Rude/Disrespectful Behavior** | Zoning Out/Lack of Focus | **Doesn't Try/Gives Up Easily**

Overview

Students, particularly challenging ones, can serve as a valuable source of feedback and information about the effectiveness of the classroom instruction and learning environment. In many classrooms, the feedback about growth, progress, and effectiveness flows only from the teacher to the student. This intervention asks for students to complete a **Course Evaluation** for the purpose of providing feedback to the teacher.

Putting It All Together

Although this intervention is often used with all students, it can be particularly powerful with students who challenge authority or have difficult, overt behaviors. Before using the intervention, it is helpful to create a worksheet or handout that lists questions or comments to rank on a Likert-type scale. Talk with the student and use an **Engaging Frame** such as "Becky, my goal is to become a better teacher, and I couldn't think of anyone better than you to give me some feedback about how I teach." Ask the student to provide feedback on questions or statements such as the following:

My teacher provides clear directions.   1   2   3   4   5

My teacher cares about me.   1   2   3   4   5

The lessons and activities are fun.   1   2   3   4   5

Students are treated fairly in class.   1   2   3   4   5

My teacher is organized.   1   2   3   4   5

Grades are fair and accurate.   1   2   3   4   5

Tips and Variations

- Depending on the student, consider including some open-ended questions, such as "One thing I would change about this class is _____."

- **Course Evaluations** are powerful because they can open a line of communication, but the feedback should never be used as a punishment or as a way to make the child feel guilty if he or she provided negative ratings or comments.

DESCRIBE THE REQUEST

| Blurting Out in Whole Group | Side Talking | Rude/ Disrespectful Behavior | Zoning Out/ Lack of Focus | Doesn't Try/ Gives Up Easily |

Overview

When teachers **Describe the Request**, they should use specific nouns and verbs to help students understand exactly what is expected of them.

Putting It All Together

Vague requests often leave students feeling uncertain and insecure about the teacher's expectations. Instead of describing the inappropriate student *behavior*, which can come across as nagging ("You haven't even started to work on your project yet!"), state the replacement behavior using as many descriptive words as necessary to help the students understand their responsibility. For example say, "Leslie, please begin working immediately on the first question on page nineteen. It asks you to explain the role of the executive branch in creating a budget for the government. Some of that information is on the chart I handed out a few minutes ago." Describing the request in specific terms will help decrease, and possibly eliminate, student confusion and off-task behavior that results from a lack of understanding.

Tips and Variations

- **Clear Directions**, including visual prompts and **Specific Time Frames**, can help to **Describe the Request**.

- Teachers should always be aware of the tone of voice they use when talking with students. As much as possible, avoid sounding annoyed, hostile, or agitated when describing the request.

- **Describe the Request** is very powerful for teachers who tend to find themselves making generic, judgmental statements about student behaviors, such as "Get to work," "Shape up," or "Work harder."

- When students are off task, avoid asking questions that begin with *why*. Questions such as "Why aren't you working on your assignment?" can come across as an accusation and often prompt students to lie or make excuses for their behavior.

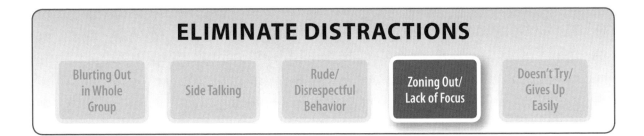

Overview

Classrooms can be over-stimulating environments with all their posters, visual images, movement, people, and constant activity. For some students, one of the best things a teacher can do is reduce or **Eliminate Distractions** to help the students focus on the learning task.

Putting It All Together

Teachers should be thoughtful when developing the classroom atmosphere, environment, and tone. A classroom that is too cluttered, overly noisy, or lacking organization may cause a student to become easily distracted and disengaged. It is imperative for teachers to reflect on the classroom environment and consider how it impacts students' learning and their ability to focus. When assisting distractible students, consider things such as the desk arrangements, locations of supplies and materials, work stations or common areas, and doors or windows. In addition to reflecting on the classroom environment, assist students with organizing their own work spaces. Help them to discover what items, behaviors, or situations are distracting, and offer them tools such as **Headphones** or a **Private Office**.

Tips and Variations

- Teachers should **Be the Model** for their students and keep their work spaces and desks clean and free of clutter.

- Minimize the number of posters, word walls, and other materials necessary for a particular unit or subject area.

- The goal is always to instill habits, thought processes, and skills in the students. Therefore, in addition to pointing out what things may be a distraction, encourage self-reflection, challenge the students to consider what may offer distractions, help them to brainstorm solutions, or ask them to create **Personal Goals**.

Overview

Simple, brief movement activities can serve as valuable classroom tools that can **Energize** (or re-energize) students, help to increase focus, and add an element of fun to the classroom.

Putting It All Together

Many students, as well as many adults, have difficulty staying focused for lengthy periods of time. Physical activities such as **Energizers** stimulate the brain and prepare students for learning. When students are low on energy, they will likely struggle to focus and remain on task. In those cases, utilize specific, short movement activities that get students out of their seats and moving around the room. Quick and simple games such as Simon Says, a ball toss, or stretching exercises will invigorate students and add the energy needed to be able to refocus on the learning tasks. Some administrators may expect that all movement activities have an academic focus. In those cases, combine the **Energizer** with content-focused questions or prompts. For example, place whiteboards on students' desks and provide them with a prompt or a question. When students have solved the problem, have them walk/skip/jump to another location in the room. Then call out a new problem, question, or prompt. This allows the students to practice content knowledge and become energized at the same time.

Tips and Variations

● **Energizers** do not need to be lengthy to be effective. A walk around the room, a **Stand and Stretch**, or switching seats will be effective.

● Before using movement interventions, reflect on the room setup to ensure that it is conducive to movement and **Energizers**.

ENGAGING FRAMES

Blurting Out in Whole Group | Side Talking | Rude/ Disrespectful Behavior | **Zoning Out/ Lack of Focus** | **Doesn't Try/ Gives Up Easily**

Overview

An **Engaging Frame** is a statement that focuses attention and helps students to understand why they should participate, complete a task, or engage in the learning.

Putting It All Together

The need to understand the rationale for participation is strong in some of our most challenging students. As a result, teachers should use **Engaging Frames** to create an intentional bias or predisposition toward listening and focusing. That is, there are certain statements that create a natural curiosity and cause students to listen differently. **Engaging Frames** can be questions, statistics, scenarios, stories, or personal experiences. Examples include the following:

- Has this ever happened to anyone?
- A recent survey found that 78 percent of all middle-school students believe this.
- Let me tell you something very strange that happened to me yesterday.
- How many of you have ever thought this before?
- Check this out; this is really interesting.
- I'm about to tell you something so important that you'll thank me later.
- Let's try an experiment. I'm not sure how it will turn out, but let's give it a shot.
- I have good news and I have bad news.
- Would you like to know the secret to getting good grades in this class?

Tips and Variations

- "This will be on the test" is an example of a frame that will be effective for some students. However, many of our most challenging students do not care about tests, and if used too often, this statement will lose its power.

- **Engaging Frames** can be strengthened with the use of visuals, current events, or real-life situations that are relevant to students.

- When an **Engaging Frame** is used effectively, the results will be immediate. You'll notice a change in the postures, attitudes, and attention of students.

EXTEND AN INVITATION

Blurting Out in Whole Group | Side Talking | Rude/ Disrespectful Behavior | Zoning Out/ Lack of Focus | Doesn't Try/ Gives Up Easily

Overview

Just about everyone appreciates a genuine invitation to participate in something meaningful or fun. Some students respond to a heartfelt invitation by the teacher to participate in the learning task or classroom activities.

Putting It All Together

This intervention relies on a one-on-one conversation between the student and teacher about the importance of participation. However, it doesn't stop at merely inviting a student to participate. It provides the student with specific *ways* to participate. During a discussion with the student, express a genuine concern and desire for the student to participate. Outline some of the strategies, tasks, or objectives of the class time, and express a belief in his or her ability to positively participate. If needed, **Ramp Up Relevance** and explain how the student's participation is needed and valued. Provide the student with a certain job or specific task to complete during the lesson. For example, the teacher may ask the student to track the number of times questions were asked, what the average wait time was during questioning, or how often the teacher responded to a student question with a direct answer.

Tips and Variations

● This intervention works well when combined with **A Head Start**, **5-Minute Focus Group**, or **Planted Questions**.

● Consider the analogy of a party. When considering accepting an invitation to a party, most individuals want to know things such as these: What kind of party is it? Who else will be at the party? Do I like those other people? Will I be expected to bring anything? What will we do at the party? How will I be expected to behave at the party? When those questions are answered positively, the likelihood of accepting the invitation increases.

Overview

A direct look and brief **Eye Contact** from a teacher to a student can be a powerful yet simple intervention. When used effectively, it can be a quick, unobtrusive intervention that will help students to refocus or change behavior.

Putting It All Together

Eye Contact, not to be confused with The Teacher Look, serves as a personal connection and an acknowledgment of a student's behavior, status, or actions. Often, teachers who use The Teacher Look intend to send an overt, negative, and sometimes angry message that conveys "Knock it off or you're going to be in big trouble!" Effective **Eye Contact**, on the other hand, can be used both to acknowledge off-task behavior and to demonstrate that the teacher has noticed on-task, productive behavior. When a student has done something worth acknowledging, either positive or negative, briefly establish **Eye Contact**, followed by a nod, thumbs-up, redirection, or a statement. This intervention demonstrates to students that the teacher knows what is happening in the classroom.

Tips and Variations

- If a student fails to respond to **Eye Contact**, consider adding **Proximity**. Both are interventions that take little effort but can have big results.

- Consider combining **Eye Contact** with **Communicate with Home**, **Compliments and Congratulations**, or **Victory List**.

- Be careful not to maintain **Eye Contact** for too long, as it may make students feel uncomfortable or send an unintended message.

5-MINUTE FOCUS GROUP

| Blurting Out in Whole Group | Side Talking | Rude/ Disrespectful Behavior | Zoning Out/ Lack of Focus | Doesn't Try/ Gives Up Easily |

Overview

This intervention allows the teacher to gain valuable insight and feedback from the student about the student's perceptions, ideas, and suggestions regarding lessons, instructional strategies, or the classroom environment.

Putting It All Together

Set aside a few minutes to ask the student about his or her opinion of a topic, lesson, or unit that will be taught in the near future. Typically done in private, the discussion is meant to genuinely gauge a student's interest in the content or methods that will be the focus of the lesson. Seek the student's opinions to gain insight into how the lesson, strategies, or focus can be improved. For example, the teacher may say, "Lisa, tomorrow I will be introducing a lesson on long division. I know that sometimes students struggle to see the importance of long division, especially when we have calculators. I have a few ideas about how I should start the lesson, but I'd really like to get your ideas. Should I start the lesson by showing a video clip, doing a KWL chart, or showing examples on the board?" After gaining the student's opinions, incorporate those ideas into the lesson.

Tips and Variations

- Depending on the age of the student and his or her sensitivity to peers, the teacher could acknowledge the student's contributions to the class. However, if the lesson is not successful or if it's not well received by the class, avoid publicly acknowledging the student who participated in the **5-Minute Focus Group**.

- Regardless of whether the student is publicly acknowledged, this intervention helps build the teacher's relationship with the student as well as the student's confidence that he or she has valuable ideas to contribute.

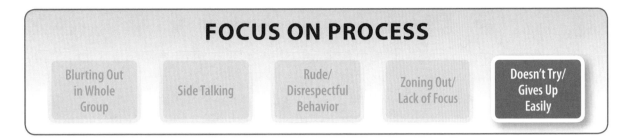

Overview

Some reluctant or hesitant students do not respond well to extrinsic motivation in the form of grades, rewards, or earned privileges. Despite that, many teachers insist on finding the "thing" that will motivate these students to put forth more effort. However, many students respond well when the focus is shifted from the outcome of a task to the process of learning.

Putting It All Together

When interacting with and encouraging students, **Focus on Process** by showing the student how participation, effort, and completion of tasks will result in *personal* growth. Focus less on the final outcome or product, which is typically centered on grades, points, or achievement, and spotlight how the process of learning and participating is personally relevant, fun, or meaningful. Essentially, the focus is less on what students get or achieve and more on what they will personally experience during the process of learning. This can be strengthened when teachers utilize student interests and create experiences that students find appealing. For example, for a student who is interested in art and drawing, point out how much he or she will enjoy the process of learning about the content through drawing.

Tips and Variations

- **Focus on Process** can be enhanced when teachers **Increase Feedback**, **Ramp Up Relevance**, and use **Engaging Frames**.

- As students gain more confidence and are willing to take more risks, help them to see the connection between the process of learning (and their participation) and the final outcome.

Overview

A small token of appreciation in the form of a tangible gift can send a powerful and positive message to challenging students.

Putting It All Together

Most students appreciate gifts, especially when they are unexpected. As a method to connect with a challenging student, giving a tangible, inexpensive token or artifact can send the message that the student is valued and appreciated. The giving of a gift sends a simple but powerful message: "I saw this and I thought it would be something you'd like." For example, the teacher may know that the student loves Legos. The teacher happens to see a free catalog, magazine, or article about Lego building and picks it up for the student. The cost is low but the benefits of the gift may be priceless. A student's response to the gift may be gratitude translated into more productivity in the classroom, increased respectful behavior, and/or increased self-esteem. However, don't be offended if the student doesn't get excited over the gift. Some students are not as overtly thankful as the teacher expects or anticipates that they will be.

Tips and Variations

- The gift should not be given with the intent to bribe or manipulate. The purpose is to deepen trust, increase communication, and instill confidence in the student. The gift should not be followed with conditions, threats, or guilt.

- Remember that the gift does not need to be costly. Often it is something small and inexpensive that makes the most impact. A pack of playing cards, a toy from a Happy Meal, an old magazine, or a stuffed animal you won at the state fair are all items that can be used as gifts for students to let them know that you are thinking of them.

- When considering the use of this intervention, consult with your administrator or school leader. Some districts may have policies governing the giving and receiving of gifts.

GIVE A JOB

Blurting Out in Whole Group | Side Talking | **Rude/ Disrespectful Behavior** | Zoning Out/ Lack of Focus | Doesn't Try/ Gives Up Easily

Overview

Typically it is only the "good" kids who are given the opportunity to be in charge of materials, given special duties, or granted the privilege of taking on classroom leadership roles. This intervention gives challenging students the opportunity to demonstrate leadership and cooperation and to serve as models of expected behavior.

Putting It All Together

Most classrooms have duties, tasks, and housekeeping jobs that students can take responsibility for. Those jobs may include handing out materials, collecting completed assignments, tutoring peers, holding doors open, or caring for a class pet. When considering which job to give to a challenging student, take into account the nature of the student's behavior and provide a job or task that he or she can complete with a high level of success. Since success builds motivation, ensure that the student understands his or her responsibility and provide the student with a chance to practice the new job in a safe environment. In addition, many challenging students struggle to put into words their frustration, regret, or remorse after they have done something inappropriate. When teachers **Give a Job** to students, it helps them to do something overt and obvious to show that they are sorry and want things to improve. For example, the teacher may say, "I know you feel bad about what happened, but you may not be quite ready to talk about it. Until then, you could do me a favor by collecting all the books and placing them on the counter."

Tips and Variations

- When considering which job to give to a challenging student, ask the student's opinion and seek his or her ideas about which jobs are most appealing.

- **Give a Job** can be combined with **Communicate with Home**, **Rating Scales**, **Track the Lesson**, or **Victory List**.

GRAPH THE RESULTS

| Blurting Out in Whole Group | Side Talking | Rude/ Disrespectful Behavior | Zoning Out/ Lack of Focus | Doesn't Try/ Gives Up Easily |

Overview

Most students benefit from a visual representation of their academic and behavioral strengths and needs. Graphing the results of improvement will help the students to visualize their growth and take ownership of their learning progress.

Putting It All Together

Meet with the student privately in order to discuss goals, behavioral expectations, and methods for improvement. Explain that you are going to work together to keep track of the number of times he or she exhibits an expected positive behavior. For example, you may say, "Max, we've been working this year on being polite and courteous with the other students in the class. We are going to start a graph to record the number of times each day that you are polite and courteous to other students." Provide the student with a method for recording the behavior (see **Behavior Tracking**) and demonstrate how to create a simple graph that shows the student's growth.

Tips and Variations

- Keep the graphs in a folder in order to show student growth over time.

- Sometimes there will be no positive growth to graph. Those cases provide an excellent opportunity to talk with the student about changes, expectations, and adjustments that he or she should make. After all, the person who analyzes the data owns it.

- When positive growth occurs, allow the student the opportunity to share the graphs with other key adults in the school, such as the principal or PE teacher.

- Use the graphs and data to **Communicate with Home**, to create **Personal Goals**, or in combination with a **Victory List**.

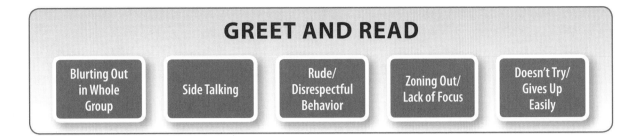

GREET AND READ

| Blurting Out in Whole Group | Side Talking | Rude/ Disrespectful Behavior | Zoning Out/ Lack of Focus | Doesn't Try/ Gives Up Easily |

Overview

Some students come to school with the weight of the world on their shoulders. They may be feeling stressed, anxious, or fearful because of something that happened at home, at the bus stop, or during another class. Teachers should make a habit of greeting each student every day and reading his or her facial expressions, body language, and attitude.

Putting It All Together

As students enter the class, stand at the door, greet students, and "read" their emotional states. One of the goals is to catch any problem behaviors or potential attitudes *before* they enter the classroom. By observing the behavior at the door, teachers are setting themselves and their students up for a successful and productive class period. However, the **Greet and Read** intervention is not just for overt, difficult attitudes from rude or disrespectful students. Some shy, reluctant, or unsuccessful students will benefit from a quick informal interaction that communicates the message "It's good to see you, and I'm glad you are in my class."

Tips and Variations

- Have a plan for what to do when a student has had a bad day. Merely telling a student to "leave problems at the door" won't likely change the student's mood or outlook.

- Although it can be difficult to stand at the door each day because of the myriad of tasks to be completed during transition times, make it a priority to first interact with students in order to set them up for success.

- Consider that many of the most challenging students receive negative feedback and messages from adults from the moment they wake up in the morning. As a result, they may enter the classroom expecting to be scolded, reprimanded, or corrected. In those cases, it is most important not only to **Greet and Read** but also to offer **Compliments and Congratulations** in an effort to help the students experience a positive beginning to class.

HEADPHONES

| Blurting Out in Whole Group | Side Talking | Rude/ Disrespectful Behavior | Zoning Out/ Lack of Focus | Doesn't Try/ Gives Up Easily |

Overview

Headphones can be an effective tool to help block out surrounding noise in the classroom. They can help students focus on a task while giving them a physical tool to ignore outside distractions.

Putting It All Together

No matter how structured and supportive the classroom environment is, there are times when the noise, movement, and activity can be too distracting for some students. It is often during times of independent or small-group work that children become distracted by all the activity in the classroom. During those times, offer students the opportunity to wear **Headphones** as a method to tune out those distractions. They serve as a noise buffer that helps students to ignore those around them and work on the task at hand. When background noise is minimized, students are able to be more focused and productive. In addition, the **Headphones** serve as a visual and **Concrete Reminder** to remain focused on their work.

Tips and Variations

- Inexpensive, cheaply made headphones will work perfectly for this intervention. Since the goal is not to eliminate all background noise, they do not even have to be plugged into an electronic device.

- Set up rules and procedures for when students can use the **Headphones** and where to store them when they are not in use.

- **Headphones** also serve as a reminder to other students not to bother or interact with the student who is wearing them.

HUMOR

| Blurting Out in Whole Group | Side Talking | Rude/ Disrespectful Behavior | Zoning Out/ Lack of Focus | Doesn't Try/ Gives Up Easily |

Overview

Jokes, riddles, stories, and celebrations create an engaging and enjoyable classroom atmosphere. Effective use of **Humor** can motivate students, create group bonding, ease tense situations, foster positive student-teacher relationships, and reduce stress.

Putting It All Together

You don't have to be a stand-up comedian to effectively use **Humor** with challenging students. You can use **Humor** effectively in the following ways:

- Use funny anecdotes as examples in lessons as a way to focus attention.
- Use jokes or one-liners to diffuse tense situations.
- Find funny stories or examples of humorous endings to difficult situations.
- Be willing to laugh at yourself and your mistakes; don't take yourself too seriously.
- Begin the day with a laugh, quote of the day, or story.
- Place humorous quotes, signs, etc. around the room.
- Incorporate **Humor**, jokes, or stories into the daily morning routine (e.g., Joke of the Day).

Tips and Variations

- Sarcasm and **Humor** should not be confused. Sarcasm has no place in the classroom, even with older students who seem to understand it. In fact, sarcasm can have the opposite impact on the classroom environment. Sarcasm is commonly used as a student management technique, but it is highly inappropriate in the classroom.
- Consider combining **Humor** with **Greet and Read** or **Solicit Good Intentions**.
- Remember that an individual's sense of humor evolves over time. Some students, particularly older ones, misuse humor, rely on crude or negative humor, or tell jokes that are inappropriate. In addition, boys seem to find unsophisticated, crude behavior especially funny. In those cases, use the opportunity to teach students about the power of humor and what types of jokes, pranks, and comedy are appropriate.

I MESSAGES

Blurting Out in Whole Group | Side Talking | Rude/ Disrespectful Behavior | Zoning Out/ Lack of Focus | Doesn't Try/ Gives Up Easily

Overview

I Messages help students to see how their actions impact others around them without the use of accusatory or argumentative language.

Putting It All Together

I Messages generally follow a pattern such as "When you _____, I feel _____ because...." An example of a teacher **I Message** is "When you talk out of turn in class, I feel frustrated because I have to stop teaching to remind you of the correct procedure." However, it is an intervention that teachers can implement to help their students successfully communicate their thoughts and feeling to another teacher or peer. **I Messages** help to facilitate meaningful dialogue and can de-escalate a problem that is occurring in the classroom. An example of a student-to-student **I Message** is "When you didn't talk to me in class, I felt hurt because I thought we were friends." **I Messages** can be used as a problem-solving strategy that gives students and teachers a **Sentence Starter** to help communicate more effectively.

Tips and Variations

- An **I Message** can be followed by a request for a replacement behavior. For example, a teacher may say, "When you talk out of turn in class, I feel disrespected because the rules of my class are being broken. From now on, I would like you to raise your hand when you would like to participate."

- Students may lack the vocabulary necessary to express their feelings appropriately. It is important to teach students "feeling" words that will help them express themselves in a respectful and acceptable manner.

IF-THEN STATEMENTS

| Blurting Out in Whole Group | Side Talking | Rude/ Disrespectful Behavior | Zoning Out/ Lack of Focus | Doesn't Try/ Gives Up Easily |

Overview

If-Then Statements are clear, unthreatening, and concise phrases that help students to understand what is expected of them and the possible outcome if they decide not to follow through with the expectation.

Putting It All Together

Teachers use **If-Then Statements** to help their students to understand classroom rules, procedures, and behavioral expectations. Using specific, concrete terms with precise time frames and **Clear Directions**, a teacher can express his or her expectations for an outcome or behavior. An example of this is "If the profanity continues, then _____ will happen." Make sure the "then" part of the statement is not said with anger or sarcasm and doesn't focus solely on punishment. When the focus is solely on punishment, it raises fear and anxiety and may actually decrease a student's ability to focus or think clearly. **If-Then Statements** can also be used in a positive way, with the teacher focusing the "then" portion on any privileges that may be earned.

Tips and Variations

- When redirecting challenging students, teachers themselves often experience strong emotions. As is the case with most interventions, you should deliver **If-Then Statements** with a calm voice, neutral body language, and an expectation that the student will make good choices.

- Remember to ensure that the "then" consequence is something that can be and will be followed up on. Students will quickly catch on when teachers fail to follow through on statements.

- Combine **If-Then Statements** with **Be Brief, Be Positive, Be Gone**; **Check-In Statements**; or **I Messages**.

INCREASE FEEDBACK

| Blurting Out in Whole Group | Side Talking | Rude/ Disrespectful Behavior | Zoning Out/ Lack of Focus | Doesn't Try/ Gives Up Easily |

Overview

All students, even challenging ones, have a desire for feedback and knowledge about their progress, growth, and status. Feedback is accurate information about a student's performance and should not be confused with praise, blame, or advice. In this context, effective feedback helps challenging students get a clear picture of their status without worrying about blame, ridicule, or embarrassment.

Putting It All Together

Feedback and advice are concepts that are often confused by teachers and adults. Feedback is a description of performance measured against a specified target while advice is what a person might do to improve or honor the feedback. For example, if the assignment is to work on an independent writing project and a student is off task, many teachers will say something such as "You need to go back to your seat and start writing." That statement is not feedback, but advice. Feedback is generally not evaluative or directive, but descriptive. In that example, effective feedback may be "Right now you are out of your seat, and I can see other students are being distracted." Effective feedback is timely and prompt in nature, specific and descriptive for the individual, simple and straightforward, and useful to the individual.

Tips and Variations

- Praise should not be confused with feedback. Praise alone is typically evaluative and focused on what the teacher liked, appreciated, or valued. While praise can help students feel better, it rarely helps them to improve. Teachers who tend to praise a lot should consider following every praise statement with a specific description of the qualities that are praiseworthy.

- Teachers can combine **Increase Feedback** with **Be Brief, Be Positive, Be Gone; If-Then Statements**; or **What You Could Have Said Was**.

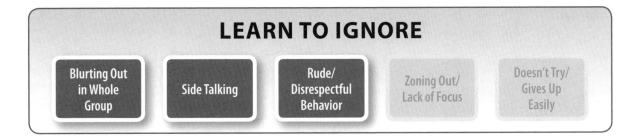

LEARN TO IGNORE

| Blurting Out in Whole Group | Side Talking | Rude/ Disrespectful Behavior | Zoning Out/ Lack of Focus | Doesn't Try/ Gives Up Easily |

Overview

Ignoring certain minor misbehaviors, even if the violations are technically against the rules, can actually serve to strengthen the classroom culture and increase trust with some students.

Putting It All Together

Some students constantly have their negative behaviors pointed out to them in school. Our most challenging students have even their most minor infractions labeled, made public, and scrutinized. However, there may be cases in which minor, off-task *but undisruptive* behavior could be ignored. When considering which behaviors to address and which to ignore, take into account the present state of the class and the impact that behavior is having on other students. If the behavior is technically against the rules but not disrupting other students, it may be a candidate for ignoring. For example, if a child gets out of his or her seat without permission to get needed supplies, but no other student in the room is impacted by the violation, it would be wise to **Learn to Ignore** that incident. In that case, a verbal redirection by the teacher could actually result in more off-task behavior within the class. Some teachers express concern that ignoring minor behavior will only encourage other students to do the same. In most cases, this doesn't happen. The teacher's practice of ignoring inappropriate behavior that is minor but non-disruptive could actually serve as a model for other students because they will learn that not every behavior needs to be noticed, commented on, or addressed.

Tips and Variations

- Examples of behaviors that may be candidates to be ignored include whispering (particularly after unclear directions or long assignments), chewing gum, rolling the eyes, blurting out answers, sitting incorrectly in a chair or on the floor, and fidgeting.

LIKELY BEFORE UNLIKELY

Blurting Out in Whole Group · Side Talking · Rude/Disrespectful Behavior · Zoning Out/Lack of Focus · Doesn't Try/Gives Up Easily

Overview

Teachers can greatly enhance on-task and cooperative behavior in students by asking them to complete **Likely Before Unlikely** tasks or actions. That is, the timing of the request is a factor in ultimate compliance.

Putting It All Together

Consider how dolphins in captivity are trained to jump out of the water over ropes and obstacles. The trainer first leaves the rope on the bottom of the tank and rewards the animal with a fish each time it swims over it. The trainer then periodically raises the rope, rewarding the dolphin each time until ultimately the animal is jumping out of the water. With this in mind, when needing to redirect students, first ask them to complete a task or job that they find enjoyable and that they are *likely to do*. For example, ask a sociable but talkative student to help by organizing papers, running an errand, or helping another student. Since these are tasks the student will likely agree to do, follow those with a request to focus on an academic task. The teacher may say, "Thank you for doing me those favors. Now please return to your desk to complete the rest of your reading assignment." Some students may need to be asked to complete several likely behaviors before they will respond positively to the unlikely behavior. The goal is to get students to be productive, to respond positively, and to have a helpful mindset before they are asked to do an unlikely behavior.

Tips and Variations

● This intervention works well in conjunction with **Be Brief, Be Positive, Be Gone**; **Chunk Tasks**; **Give a Job**; or **Solicit Good Intentions**.

● It is important to know the motivation, behavior patterns, and habits of individual students before using this intervention. Some students get stuck in negative mindsets and have difficulty seeing other perspectives. For a suggestion on how to get students out of negative mindsets, see **Positive Self-Talk**.

LOOKS LIKE, SOUNDS LIKE, FEELS LIKE

Blurting Out in Whole Group

Side Talking

Rude/ Disrespectful Behavior

Zoning Out/ Lack of Focus

Doesn't Try/ Gives Up Easily

Overview

The **Looks Like, Sounds Like, Feels Like** intervention offers teachers and students alike the chance to clarify expectations and state them in concrete terms so that everyone has a clear understanding of what proper classroom participation looks like, what it sounds like, and what it feels like.

Putting It All Together

This intervention is particularly useful for helping students understand abstract behaviors. Students are often implored to *do their best* and *try harder* only to find the teacher's expectations are very different from their own. Nowhere is this conflict more evident than in the classroom. Teachers often tell students to behave in terms that are abstract and open to interpretation. For example, when a teacher tells the students to "be nice," a student could reasonably reply, depending on his or her background and experiences, "I was being nice: I didn't hit him!"

Provide students with a handout that has three columns: one labeled **Looks Like**, another labeled **Sounds Like**, and another labeled **Feels Like**. At the top of the sheet, list *one* specific behavior, such as working positively with a partner. In partnership with the student(s), brainstorm the specific behaviors that you expect when students are in that situation. Students may list *keeping hands to self*, *sharing supplies such as markers*, and *using words like* please *and* thank you. The first two columns—**Looks Like** and **Sounds Like**—focus on external behaviors that can be seen and measured by both the student and the teacher. The **Feels Like** column lists how students would expect to feel if they were meeting expectations. For example, students may say that they feel *more confident* or *happy* if they were working positively with their peers.

Tips and Variations

- Some teachers have chosen to use this method with the entire class as a way to clarify rules at the beginning of the year.

MINIMIZE ANXIETY

Blurting Out in Whole Group | Side Talking | **Rude/ Disrespectful Behavior** | Zoning Out/ Lack of Focus | **Doesn't Try/ Gives Up Easily**

Overview

Anxiety is the body's response to threat, harm, or stress because of apprehension or uncertainty about the future. Many challenging students do not have the tools or skills to deal appropriately with anxiety. When teachers use specific, overt interventions to **Minimize Anxiety** and teach ways to deal with stress, they are providing students with lifelong skills.

Putting It All Together

Not all stress and anxiety should be viewed as a bad thing; it is the behaviors that result when students are anxious or stressed that can be problematic. There are two ways to assist students who are prone to anxious behaviors. First, reduce the reliance on grades, extrinsic motivators, rewards, and lectures. In particular, attempt to eliminate the use of the pronouns *I*, *you*, and *me* and statements that could be interpreted as a threat. For example, "You'd better get to work or I might have to call home again. You don't want me to do that, do you?" could be interpreted by the student as a threat. Second, teach students specific ways to handle stress and anxiety. Deep breathing, stretching, **Positive Self-Talk**, physical movement, **Humor**, and **Stories** are all effective ways to deal with stress. In addition, during one-on-one discussions with students, seek to understand which situations, events, or people are likely to produce anxiety.

Tips and Variations

- **A Head Start**, **Planted Questions**, and **Teacher-Approved Toys** can help to reduce stress and anxiety.

- Merely telling students to "chill out" or "relax" doesn't work. In fact, statements such as these may actually increase stress when they are made in a threatening or sarcastic tone. Students need to be taught specifically how to manage stressful situations.

OFFER THE DOOR

Blurting Out in Whole Group | Side Talking | **Rude/ Disrespectful Behavior** | Zoning Out/ Lack of Focus | Doesn't Try/ Gives Up Easily

Overview

This intervention allows a challenging student the opportunity to gain composure, collect his or her thoughts, or save face in a way that allows the teacher to address a problem behavior while protecting a child's dignity.

Putting It All Together

This intervention should not be confused with the forced removal of a child from the classroom. Certainly there are situations when a student needs to be removed, but the **Offer the Door** intervention is voluntary on the student's part and is done in partnership between the teacher and the child. When a student is unable to focus or improve behavior, privately offer the student the opportunity to run an errand, take a bathroom break, or leave the classroom for a specific purpose. Acknowledge the student's situation or frustration and his or her current inability to focus. Provide the student with a chance to temporarily leave the classroom with the understanding that he or she will return within a specific time and with a change in attitude or demeanor. This intervention should only be used *before* a situation escalates and only when the teacher is sure that the child will return. In other words, don't **Offer the Door** to a child who is a flight risk. The goal is to provide the student the opportunity to deal with an issue and then return to class with an increased ability to focus and participate.

Tips and Variations

- **Offer the Door** should not to be used when either the teacher or student is angry, upset, or irritated. It is not the same as "Get out of the classroom" and will be effective only when all parties are calm and the teacher has a genuine concern about the student's status.

- Combine **Offer the Door** with **Questions of Concern**, **Smile**, or **Start Statements**.

- If the child chooses not to leave the room, consider **Give a Job** or use an **Engaging Frame**.

PERSONAL GOALS

| Blurting Out in Whole Group | Side Talking | Rude/ Disrespectful Behavior | Zoning Out/ Lack of Focus | Doesn't Try/ Gives Up Easily |

Overview

Motivation, participation, and behavior tend to improve when students are provided with clear objectives, coherent directions, engaging and relevant tasks, and **Personal Goals**.

Putting It All Together

Explain to the student that successful people from all walks of life create and track goals as a way to measure their progress and growth. These goals serve as motivators and yardsticks by which we can measure progress and achievement. The most powerful goals, however, are ones that are self-created. That is, they come from within and are based on one's perceived needs and desires. Work with the student to consider, brainstorm, and list both short-term and long-term goals. When the goals relate to improved classroom focus or behavior, it is best to help the student narrow the goals to a few that are achievable. The true power of **Personal Goals** is not in the creation of them but in the tracking, feedback, discussions, and success that come from meeting the goals. If appropriate, provide students with goal sheets and assist them in writing the goals using specific language and deadlines.

Tips and Variations

- Teachers can model the creation of goals for students by writing and sharing their own goals.

- Short term **Personal Goals** can be listed on a **Checklist** and tracked daily. This is especially powerful for students who need immediate feedback, and it can be motivating to check items off the list as they are accomplished.

- When **Personal Goals** are accomplished, they can be turned into a **Victory List** and sent home.

- Ensure that students do not create too many goals or create goals that are too lofty. Some students overestimate their ability, and it can be "de-motivating" to fail to reach the goals.

Overview

Many students respond well to visual images that provide support, examples, and evidence of expected appropriate behavior. **Photographic Evidence** is an intervention that uses images and pictures to show and model expected behavior.

Putting It All Together

Gather images and pictures that demonstrate expected classroom behaviors, such as taking turns, sharing materials, getting attention, etc. Compile those pictures in a folder or envelope, or tape them onto the surface of a desk for individual students. Include a brief description or title for each photograph, such as "The proper way to line up." Some teachers use plastic picture inserts, the type that come in wallets, and give one to each student. When providing direction, support, or guidance to students, refer to the **Photographic Evidence** in addition to providing verbal redirections or reprimands.

Tips and Variations

● When selecting which photographs to include, ensure that they include positive emotional scenes and images. As humans, we have the tendency to take on the emotions of those around us. As it turns out, emotions can be influenced by pictures and images. Therefore, ensure that the images have positive emotional messages.

● Some teachers choose to create posters of **Photographic Evidence** and place those next to the rules that are posted in the classroom.

● Some entire schools have adopted this intervention and included images and pictures throughout the campus that show expectations for such things as walking in the hallways, preparing for lunch, and delivering information to the front office.

● Consider taking pictures of your students and using them as examples of the **Photographic Evidence**.

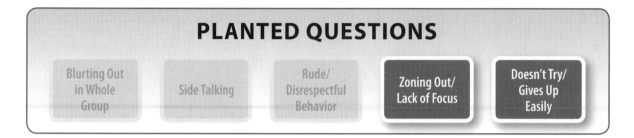

PLANTED QUESTIONS

| Blurting Out in Whole Group | Side Talking | Rude/ Disrespectful Behavior | Zoning Out/ Lack of Focus | Doesn't Try/ Gives Up Easily |

Overview

This intervention encourages students to participate in whole-group and small-group activities by offering them the opportunity to consider their thoughts, answers, and ideas to questions *before* they are asked by the teacher.

Putting It All Together

The goal is for students to become comfortable participating in discussions, with the ultimate aim of giving them the confidence to speak for themselves. Before the lesson, talk privately with the student(s) and explain that you have created an easy way for students to participate in class or group discussions. Tell the student the topic of the lesson and then give him or her a list of the questions that will be asked during the lesson or small-group activity. Ask the student to indicate which question(s) he or she would like to answer and provide clarification, if needed. Depending on the confidence level of the student, you may give actual answers or hints. Again, the goal is to build confidence in students and help them to take the first steps toward positive participation.

Tips and Variations

- The teacher may also choose to provide the student with a sample **Sentence Starter** to use when answering the question.

- Some teachers wonder about the response from other students if they discover that certain students have been given the questions ahead of time. This seems a little like cheating. Furthermore, if the actual answers are also given, it would seem that these students have been given an unfair advantage. It is important to keep in mind that the goal is positive classroom participation, not assessment. The students are not being given answers to test questions, nor will they necessarily be given a better grade on any assignment.

POSITIVE SELF-TALK

Blurting Out in Whole Group | Side Talking | **Rude/ Disrespectful Behavior** | Zoning Out/ Lack of Focus | **Doesn't Try/ Gives Up Easily**

Overview

Positive Self-Talk is an intervention that helps students to replace negative internal dialogues with positive ones. For most of us, the internal conversation we have with ourselves helps us to plan, solve problems, and think through options or scenarios. For some students, however, that internal conversation is primarily a negative one. Many challenging students come from negative environments and are constantly bombarded with negative, hurtful, and unproductive comments. As a result, they internalize that negativity in their self-talk.

Putting It All Together

Explain to the student that we all have a little voice in our heads that help us to think through and solve problems. Sometimes that voice is negative and tells us that we can't succeed, or it exaggerates how big our problems are. Tell the student that sometimes we have to "tame" that voice and replace negative thoughts with positive ones. For example, when a student feels overwhelmed with an assignment and wants to give up, have the student repeat statements such as "This is no big deal. I know this stuff" or "If I take my time and ask for help, I know I can get an excellent grade." The process of teaching students to replace negative thoughts with positive ones will take time and will at first likely have to be initiated by the teacher. Ultimately, the goal is to get students to internalize positive messages.

Tips and Variations

- Consider combining **Positive Self-Talk** with a **Concrete Reminder**, such as a special pencil, and encourage students to internally repeat statements every time they use the object.

- The ability to regulate behavior with self-talk is a skill that is developed over time. Since some of our students lack that ability, it is very important for teachers to model positive statements, use supportive nonverbal stances, and express a belief in the students' abilities.

Bryan Harris and Cassandra Goldberg

PRIVATE OFFICE

Blurting Out in Whole Group | **Side Talking** | Rude/ Disrespectful Behavior | **Zoning Out/ Lack of Focus** | Doesn't Try/ Gives Up Easily

Overview

A **Private Office** is a location in the classroom that gives students personal space, free from classroom distractions and stimuli, where they can focus and complete learning tasks.

Putting It All Together

The **Private Office** should be a location in the room that a student can use when he or she needs to focus on a task, step away from distractions, or simply take a break. This space can be a specific place in the room, such as a chair by the teacher's desk or a desk that has been placed in the corner of the room. However, it can also be the student's own desk or work space. In order to make it more private, the student can place two manila folders up around his or her work area to make the space more closed-in and personal. This provides the benefit of a physical boundary and can also be helpful in sending messages to other students that the student needs private work time and is not to be interrupted.

Tips and Variations

● A student may use **Headphones** while in the **Private Office** to help block out surrounding noise.

● Sometimes students who are agitated or upset need to have a place that permits them time and seclusion to cool down. This gives students their own space and allows them to stay in the classroom while refocusing their energy on learning.

Overview

Proximity is the act of physically moving closer to a student who is off task with the goal of helping him or her to refocus. The presence of the teacher serves to change the current situation and often is all that is needed to help a student get back on task.

Putting It All Together

Just as drivers slow down when a police car is near, the concept of physical **Proximity** shows the power of the presence of authority to change behavior. When a student is off task or engaging in an inappropriate behavior, move closer to the student while continuing to teach the class. The mere presence of the teacher will usually alert the student and result in a change of behavior. In most cases, **Proximity** is all that is needed, but the teacher may opt to **Increase Feedback** or **Be Brief, Be Positive, Be Gone**. Note that effective **Proximity** is not the same as hovering, nagging, or threatening. It is most often a nonverbal intervention that allows the teacher to extinguish the off-task behavior while continuing to teach.

Tips and Variations

- The business world has an acronym for **Proximity**: MBWA (Managing By Walking Around).

- When setting up the physical environment of the classroom (desks, tables, chairs, storage, etc.), consider the ability to easily move around the room.

- Note that this intervention can, depending on the causes of the misbehavior, backfire when used with rude or disrespectful students. Students with those behaviors may take the teacher's presence as a threat and escalate a confrontation. As with all the interventions, carefully consider causes of misbehavior before implementing any supports.

QUESTIONS OF CONCERN

| Blurting Out in Whole Group | Side Talking | Rude/ Disrespectful Behavior | Zoning Out/ Lack of Focus | Doesn't Try/ Gives Up Easily |

Overview

A **Question of Concern** is a simple, heartfelt statement or question that acknowledges the feelings or frustrations of a student. When used well, it can break down barriers and help students to understand that assistance and support are available.

Putting It All Together

When you notice that a student is struggling to focus, to maintain positive interactions with other students, or to generally behave appropriately, ask sincere questions or make statements such as "Are you okay?" or "You don't seem yourself today; is everything all right?" or "I noticed that was a difficult situation for you. How are you holding up?" Many students will respond to an offer of assistance or support if you offer it privately, with a genuine desire to help. **Questions of Concern** communicate that the teacher notices, cares, and understands that there are times when it is difficult to focus on learning. If a student is open to suggestions, the teacher could follow up with questions such as "Do you mind if I share how other students have handled this situation?" This dialogue can help students to see alternatives and options.

Tips and Variations

- **Questions of Concern** can be combined with **Greet and Read**, **Offer the Door**, **Positive Self-Talk**, or **Private Office**.

- If the student fails to respond positively to **Questions of Concern**, he or she may just need additional time to calm down or reflect, or the student may simply need to be left alone. When students are extremely agitated, it may be appropriate to **Learn to Ignore**.

- In cases in which students made positive choices and changed their behavior, consider using a **Victory List** or **Communicate with Home**.

RAMP UP RELEVANCE

Blurting Out in Whole Group | Side Talking | **Rude/ Disrespectful Behavior** | **Zoning Out/ Lack of Focus** | **Doesn't Try/ Gives Up Easily**

Overview

In the classroom, few things are as motivating, interesting, or long-lasting as a relevant topic, subject, or issue. When teachers strive to **Ramp Up Relevance**, they see increased motivation, improved behavior, and more positive attitudes.

Putting It All Together

Creating relevant, interesting, and engaging lessons and activities is about helping students to discover connections between ideas, events, or concepts. Too often, in the rush to cover material and keep up with curricular demands, teachers bypass relevance for expediency. Some students do fine in this context and are able to make connections and meaning on their own. However, some of the most challenging students do not have the skills to connect the dots and see value, meaning, and relevance on their own. As a result of being subjected to an irrelevant curriculum, many students exhibit negative behaviors. When working with these students, make every effort to show them how the content and activities are relevant to their personal experiences, goals, and success. Utilize their personal experiences, stories, real-world applications, choices, projects, and student-to-student interactions to **Ramp Up Relevance**.

Tips and Variations

● Students of all ages are particularly interested in learning about themselves. Therefore, utilize self-assessments, learning-style inventories, and personal histories.

● In *Quantum Teaching*, Bobbi DePorter and her co-authors challenge teachers to answer WIIFM for their students—What's in it for me?

● Encourage students to discover relevance on their own by asking them questions such as "How would you use this information?" or "How does this information impact how you think about_____?"

● While all students benefit from an increased focus on relevance, this intervention is typically more effective with students who have non-impulsive behaviors.

RATING SCALES

Blurting Out in Whole Group | Side Talking | Rude/ Disrespectful Behavior | Zoning Out/ Lack of Focus | Doesn't Try/ Gives Up Easily

Overview

Rating Scales are numerical representations, typically expressed on a scale of 1–10, that communicate how students are doing behaviorally or academically in a particular area.

Putting It All Together

Rating Scales are not a one-size-fits-all strategy and should therefore be customized to fit the needs of the individual student or groups of students. The power of this intervention lies in the fact that behaviors or expectations are expressed in real, understandable, and meaningful ways for students. Consider a student who is talking too loudly and disrupting the learning of other students. Instead of issuing a "You're being too loud" type statement, consider placing a numerical value on the behavior. For example, redirect the student by saying, "On a scale of 1 to 10, with 10 being totally focused and quietly working, right now you are about a 6." As a caution, keep all ratings of behavior between 6 and 10 on a 1–10 scale. If a student is rated as a 2, although it may be accurate, the low rating could cause behavior to worsen. A 6 still shows plenty of room to improve.

Tips and Variations

- Most students are capable of rating their own actions when asked to reflect on the impact of their behavior on others. Ask, "On a scale of 1 to 10, with 10 being completely focused on your assignment, how would you rate yourself right now?" This can be done in conjunction with **Be Brief, Be Positive, Be Gone** or **Increase Feedback**.

- Students may find it useful to **Graph the Results** of their **Rating Scales**. This allows them the opportunity to visually see what areas they are making progress in and what areas they may need more support in.

RIGHT TO PASS

| Blurting Out in Whole Group | Side Talking | Rude/ Disrespectful Behavior | Zoning Out/ Lack of Focus | Doesn't Try/ Gives Up Easily |

Overview

The **Right to Pass** provides students the comfort and security they need to be able to focus on a classroom discussion without the worry of being singled out, caught off guard, or unable to articulately respond to a question.

Putting It All Together

Although participation is expected during classroom activities, there are times when it is appropriate to provide a student the opportunity to opt out of certain portions of the lesson. While all students need to be held responsible for learning and mastering the content, not all students should be forced to publicly participate in whole-class activities. Prior to the lesson, tell the student that there are certain times when he or she will have the **Right to Pass**. That is, there are times when the student can make the choice to opt out of an activity or a portion of an activity. Explain that should the student exercise the right, he or she should still listen, focus, and learn from other students in the class. The **Right to Pass** generally refers to a student's choice to participate in whole-group activities such as answering questions, publicly responding, or sharing with a partner. The student is still responsible for the content and learning; he or she is merely choosing to express knowledge in a different way.

Tips and Variations

- Since the **Right to Pass** is a *right*, a student should not be led to feel guilty for exercising that right.

- If a student opts out too often, consider using **A Head Start**, **Planted Questions**, or **Sentence Starters**.

- This intervention recognizes and values the fact that students have choices and control over their lives and empowers them to make instructional decisions for themselves.

SECRET SIGNAL

| Blurting Out in Whole Group | Side Talking | Rude/ Disrespectful Behavior | Zoning Out/ Lack of Focus | Doesn't Try/ Gives Up Easily |

Overview

A **Secret Signal** is a method to convey a private message from teacher to student. The signals and their meaning are typically known only to the teacher and the student. They are used to send a very specific message and can be used by the teacher without having to interrupt class.

Putting It All Together

This intervention is effective because it serves as a discrete method to send a message to a student that a specific behavior is noticed. Before using this intervention, discuss with the student the signal and the reason for using it. For example, for a student that has a habit of talking during whole-group lessons, explain that a **Secret Signal** will be used that is known only to the two of you. This signal can serve two purposes. Most commonly, the teacher will use the signal to get the student to redirect and improve his or her behavior. Examples of signals include tapping the bottom lip, a special look such as raised eyebrows, a nod, or holding a special item such as a pencil. The signals do not need to be elaborate and should be easy to understand. This intervention can, and should, also be utilized to recognize positive behavior. In those cases, the teacher employs the signal to show students that he or she recognizes and appreciates focused, positive behavior.

Tips and Variations

- The **Closed Fist** intervention is an example of a **Secret Signal**.

- Some students may use a **Secret Signal** as a method to communicate their needs or wants to the teacher without having to publicly proclaim a need.

- Carol Burnett used to tug on her earlobe during each of her television shows as a **Secret Signal** to her grandmother watching at home.

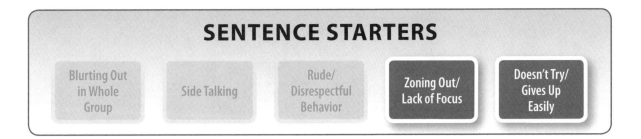

Overview

Some students struggle to select and use the appropriate words and phrases to describe their needs, ideas, and opinions. This intervention provides students with a method to put their thoughts into words.

Putting It All Together

Sentence Starters are literally the words and phrases that students should use to begin summarizing their thoughts and ideas. As a sort of mental jump start, this intervention assists students by providing them with a way to begin a verbal interaction so that they can focus on meaning instead of getting fixated on word selection. Students should be instructed to begin their sentences or discussions using the exact words provided. When used consistently, **Sentence Starters** provide students a specific, clear structure for participating in discussions. Examples of **Sentence Starters** include the following:

● In my opinion, the best thing to do would be to …

● The very first thing we need to do is …

● If we were to start over, we'd need to …

● We'll need _____ and _____ in order to start the assignment.

● This situation was frustrating/enjoyable/confusing/memorable because …

● The most important fact to know is …

● Something I don't know for sure is …

Tips and Variations

● This intervention works well in conjunction with **Planted Questions** and **What You Could Have Said Was**.

● **Sentence Starters** can be used to debrief content learning in addition to learning experiences, events, conflicts, or scenarios.

SLANT

| Blurting Out in Whole Group | Side Talking | Rude/ Disrespectful Behavior | Zoning Out/ Lack of Focus | Doesn't Try/ Gives Up Easily |

Overview

When students are expected to pay attention, focus, and listen, they need to be taught the specific expectations, body stances, and behaviors that will lead to success. **SLANT** is an acronym that is used to remind students of the proper behaviors to exhibit when listening to a speaker.

Putting It All Together

When students need to focus on a speaker, instruct them that it is time to **SLANT**. The acronym outlines five key behaviors that maximize a student's ability to pay attention, focus, and learn.

Sit Up—Instruct students how to sit and how to orient their bodies or position themselves in a way that will maximize their ability to focus.

Lean Forward—Tell students to lean slightly toward the person who is speaking.

Ask and Answer Questions—Encourage the students to be active by asking questions about the information being presented.

Nod Your Head—When the speaker makes a statement or asks a question, practice nonverbal responses such as head nods, raised eyebrows, or thumbs-up.

Track the Speaker—Inform students that they want to constantly track and watch the speaker's movements, hand motions, and non-verbals. Much of a speaker's message is delivered nonverbally.

Tips and Variations

● Use the **SLANT** reminder only in a positive way. Avoid reprimanding students or using **SLANT** to highlight what students are doing wrong. If students fail to respond to the cue appropriately, use that as an opportunity to re-teach expected behaviors.

● One variation favored by some teachers is STAR—**S**it up, **T**rack the speaker, **A**sk questions, **R**espect those around you.

SMILE

Blurting Out in Whole Group | Side Talking | Rude/Disrespectful Behavior | Zoning Out/Lack of Focus | Doesn't Try/Gives Up Easily

Overview

A simple, genuine **Smile** is one of the most powerful tools for a classroom teacher. It is not only contagious but also can reduce stress, influence mood, and encourage listening.

Putting It All Together

When a student is struggling to focus or behave appropriately, gain his or her attention and offer a genuine **Smile** followed by a repetition of the direction or a clarification of the expectation. In some cases, no verbal interaction or redirection is necessary; all it may take is an "I see you" look. A **Smile** should also be offered during times when students are on task and focused on the learning objectives. A brief **Smile** followed by "Thank you" sends the message that the child is valued and noticed.

Tips and Variations

- As an intervention, consider adding a **Smile** during **Greet and Read**, when establishing **Eye Contact** or **Proximity**, or during **Be Brief, Be Positive, Be Gone**.

- Many students are acute at noticing the differences among real, faked, and sarcastic smiles. If a genuine, heartfelt **Smile** isn't possible, consider using a different intervention.

- The old adage "Don't smile 'til Christmas" is among the worst advice ever offered to new teachers. Teachers should **Smile** often, starting from the very first second they interact with their students.

SOLICIT GOOD INTENTIONS

| Blurting Out in Whole Group | Side Talking | Rude/ Disrespectful Behavior | Zoning Out/ Lack of Focus | Doesn't Try/ Gives Up Easily |

Overview

Most people desire to behave in a way that is congruent with their stated beliefs, values, or intentions. This intervention leads teachers to **Solicit Good Intentions** from students with the purpose of getting them to commit to certain behaviors, attitudes, or thoughts.

Putting It All Together

Often combined with **Be Brief, Be Positive, Be Gone** or **Greet and Read**, this intervention involves a brief conversation between the teacher and the student that is focused on getting the student to verbalize and commit to certain positive behaviors. For example, the teacher may say, "Brody, today when we review how to use the lab equipment for our experiment, would you commit to doing your best to raise your hand when you want to answer a question?" Essentially, the teacher is asking for a pledge of good behavior. Although students may violate their pledges at times, this intervention should not be used to punish a child or to withhold privileges. Should a student not live up to the pledge, a gentle but firm reminder about his or her commitment would be appropriate when combined with encouragement and feedback.

Tips and Variations

- "Yes, I will commit to …" is a powerful statement, but it should not be coerced from the student, nor should there be a reliance on extrinsic motivators or rewards.

- **Solicit Good Intentions** works well when combined with **Communicate with Home, Rating Scales, Sentence Starters**, or **Victory Lists**.

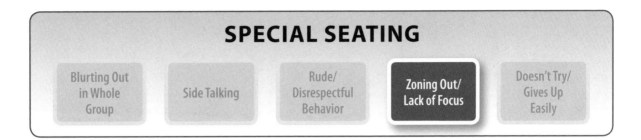

Overview

Special Seating is the act of seating a student in a location where he or she is most likely to be able to focus on the learning tasks.

Putting It All Together

Special Seating merely recognizes that students differ in their ability to focus, their need for physical movement, and the location in the classroom where they will be most productive. Just as not every employee is equally productive in an office or cubicle, not every student will be productive in the same classroom locations. For example, not all students are able to learn or focus well when sitting in a chair with their feet firmly planted on the floor. However, that is what many teachers ask their students to do. **Special Seating** provides students options that help them to remain focused on a task. When choosing *where* to seat a student, consider things such as proximity to the teacher or **Teaching Spot**; location of classroom supplies, centers, and materials; and doors or windows or other things that may be a distraction. When choosing *how* students sit, allow them options in how to orient their bodies. As long as they stay focused, on task, and non-disruptive, students should have options in how they sit in their chairs.

Tips and Variations

- Some classrooms use large exercise balls as chairs for students. The slight movement and bouncing effect helps to increase stimulation and focus.

- Another option is to securely attach a bungee cord between the legs of the chair or desk. This will give the students a footrest that also allows them to bounce their legs up and down and expend some of their energy.

SPECIFIC TIME FRAMES

| Blurting Out in Whole Group | Side Talking | Rude/ Disrespectful Behavior | Zoning Out/ Lack of Focus | Doesn't Try/ Gives Up Easily |

Overview

Specific Time Frames provide students with a clear picture of the expectations, time limits, and expected outcomes of a task or project.

Putting It All Together

Vague, unclear, or imprecise due dates and time limits are frustrating to students. An effective tool when dealing with challenging students is to provide them with specific, concrete time limits to complete tasks or assignments. As an intervention, **Specific Time Frames** set students up for success by communicating exactly what is expected of them and *when*. Instead of imploring a student, "Get to work. You don't have much time left," provide specific details about the time frame in which he or she will be held accountable. For example, say, "The first draft of this paper is due by the end of the class period. You have thirty-six minutes left. By that time, I will expect to see the completed draft, including your notes and citations." In addition to the use of verbal prompts, provide students with visual cues such as countdown timers, egg timers, stopwatches, or times written on the board. The use of these tools helps to alert students and can provide a sense of urgency needed to help students focus on the task.

Tips and Variations

- Some teachers use stress statements, such as "You have ten minutes left to complete this assignment. If you don't get it done, you are going to miss recess." These statements should be used with caution and never used for the entire class. Some students are very motivated by such statements and will work hard to meet the time limit. Other students will shut down because of the fear of losing the privilege. Therefore, use those types of statements only after considering the ability of and impact on the child.

- Consider combining **Specific Time Frames** with **Be Brief, Be Positive, Be Gone**; **Chunk Tasks**; **Compliments and Congratulations**; or **Increase Feedback**.

75 Quick and Easy Solutions to Common Classroom Disruptions

SPONGE ACTIVITIES

| Blurting Out in Whole Group | Side Talking | Rude/ Disrespectful Behavior | Zoning Out/ Lack of Focus | Doesn't Try/ Gives Up Easily |

Overview

Sponge Activities are pre-planned, quick academic tasks that are designed to "soak up" those five-to-ten minute gaps that happen in daily classroom schedules.

Putting It All Together

Even with well-planned and structured lessons, students will finish tasks at different times. Teachers often field questions such as "I'm done. Now what do I do?" These times are often fraught with inappropriate behaviors as students seek attention or find ways to fill those time gaps. During these times teachers will often respond with "Go recheck your work" or "You can have free reading time." Some students will respond well to those directives, but many challenging students will recognize that those are merely methods to get them to be quiet and leave the teacher alone. Instead, teachers should have a list of **Sponge Activities** to use with their students during these times. These activities should be directly related to the content or objectives of the lesson and should help students to solidify new information, recall past information, or make connections with important content. For example, after a student has finished with a reading assignment, the teacher may tell the student, "Write three important facts that you learned from the reading today."

Tips and Variations

- Teachers should have an easily accessible list of **Sponge Activities** that can be used in any content area. Examples include the following: List ten _____ and then rank them in order of importance. Write five sentences using the word _____. List all the _____ you can think of that start with the letter _____.

- When choosing the correct **Sponge Activities** for a specific student, refer to Bloom's Taxonomy in order to provide the appropriate level of challenge.

Overview

Allowing a quick **Stand and Stretch** break can help re-energize students and get them ready for learning.

Putting It All Together

Although movement and stretch breaks are beneficial to all students, they can be an especially powerful intervention for students who tend to lack focus or give up easily. Teachers should remain conscious of how long students have been sitting or sedentary, with the understanding that many students do not focus well when forced to sit for long periods of time. Much evidence and research suggest that physical movement helps to increase focus, motivation, and task completion. By allowing **Stand and Stretch** breaks more frequently, you enable students to increase energy, thus increasing their ability to concentrate on the task at hand for longer periods of time.

Tips and Variations

- Having students **Stand and Stretch** may help **Minimize Anxiety** for some students.

- Some teachers also elect to lead students in breathing exercises designed to relax students and decrease stress levels.

START STATEMENTS

| Blurting Out in Whole Group | Side Talking | Rude/ Disrespectful Behavior | Zoning Out/ Lack of Focus | Doesn't Try/ Gives Up Easily |

Overview

Start Statements are short, positive reminders of the teacher's expectations and serve as a clear directive about what students should *begin* doing instead of what they should *stop* doing.

Putting It All Together

Challenging students are given several directives and commands throughout the day. Many of them begin with *stop:* stop running, stop talking, stop fooling around, stop texting, and so on. Although these statements get the point across to students about what is expected of them, they may also come across as negative and sometimes harsh in tone. Instead, try to rephrase the "stop" statement as a **Start Statement**. For example, teachers may find themselves saying to students, "Stop wasting time." This statement does not guide students to effectively change their behavior to a more positive action. Instead, when the teacher feels as though the student is wasting time, the teacher can prompt the student to begin working by saying, "Please start working on question number three." By doing so, the teacher is conveying his or her expectations while remaining positive.

Tips and Variations

● A **Start Statement** can often be followed by a **Check-In Statement** if the teacher feels that the student may need to be monitored more frequently for on-task behavior.

● Consider using **Start Statements** after a **Stand and Stretch** or an **Energizer**.

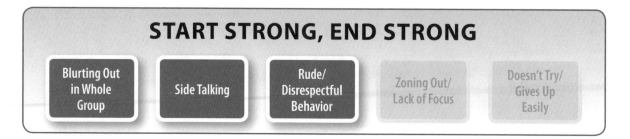

Overview

The first ten minutes and the last ten minutes of class are when many inappropriate behaviors and disruptions occur. As a result, it is very important to be organized, direct, and prepared for these times.

Putting It All Together

When planning lessons and objectives for students, give specific attention to the tasks and activities students are to complete during the first and last ten minutes of class. Understand that many students view this transition time as more casual or less important and therefore often engage in behaviors during this time that they wouldn't otherwise. Consider beginning the class with an **Engaging Frame**, a **Story**, or a specific task that they can complete on their own at their desks. During the first ten minutes, use **Proximity**, **Eye Contact**, and **Greet and Read** to interact with the students in order to get them focused and ready to learn. Do not use the first ten minutes to do administrative tasks such as attendance, lunch counts, or homework review. In some cases, it may be helpful to script, word for word, the directions you will give to the students during this time. Have all materials, handouts, books, etc. ready before students arrive. During the last ten minutes of class, engage students in activities that relate back to the learning objective and give them specific topics to discuss with partners or small groups. Use **Proximity**, **Three More Minutes, and ...**, or a **Victory List** to help students to focus during the last ten minutes.

Tips and Variations

● Contrary to popular belief, the first and last ten minutes of a time period are actually excellent times to review and teach important concepts. Because of the Primacy-Recency Effect, the brain naturally gives special attention and focus to those events, learnings, or situations that take place at the beginning and end of a time period.

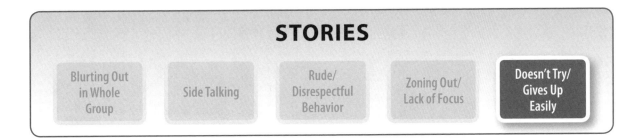

STORIES

| Blurting Out in Whole Group | Side Talking | Rude/ Disrespectful Behavior | Zoning Out/ Lack of Focus | Doesn't Try/ Gives Up Easily |

Overview

Students who tend to give up easily often have deeply imbedded, negative thought processes that, based on consistently negative experiences in school, tell them that putting forth effort or hard work is a waste of time. These students need to be provided with clear models, examples, and **Stories** that demonstrate how hard work and effort have positive results.

Putting It All Together

Knowing that success breeds motivation, privately talk with the student about his or her strengths, goals, and the areas in which he or she needs to put forth more effort. However, rather than just reprimanding or scolding students about their effort, tell them **Stories** of individuals who overcame obstacles, worked hard, and experienced the positive results of their efforts. **Stories** have the ability to plant the seeds of change and they can, over time, help to change a negative mindset. They show, in a real and memorable way, that success is achievable. The **Stories** could be personal in nature (as in the obstacles the teacher has overcome), but some of the most powerful **Stories** belong to celebrities, athletes, and historical figures. Any library will be full of biographies about individuals who overcame obstacles to experience success.

Tips and Variations

- When there is a tendency to lecture a student about poor behavior or lack of focus, consider telling a **Story** that has a moral about hard work and effort. Keep it short, to the point, and positive.

- For more information about helping students change negative mindsets to ones of hope, growth, and change, read the book *Mindset* by Carol Dweck.

- Remember that teachers need to model the ethics of hard work, effort, and positivity. The greatest story offered by teachers is told by their life and actions.

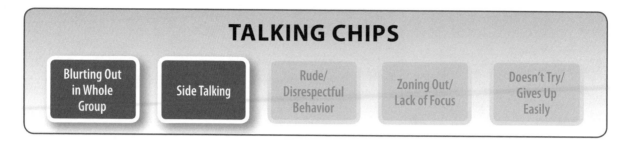

TALKING CHIPS

| Blurting Out in Whole Group | Side Talking | Rude/ Disrespectful Behavior | Zoning Out/ Lack of Focus | Doesn't Try/ Gives Up Easily |

Overview

Talking Chips can be used in large- or small-group activities as a concrete procedure for turn-taking. They are a useful tool for allowing all students to have an opportunity to answer questions or communicate their thoughts and ideas with the group.

Putting It All Together

For students who tend to talk at inappropriate times, **Talking Chips** are effective because they provide a specific structure and method for how, when, and how long to talk. The teacher gives each student a certain number of **Talking Chips**. "Chips" can be small squares of construction paper, coins, plastic shapes, poker chips, etc. The chips represent how many times a student can talk during a specified amount of time or specific activity. For example, the teacher may pose a discussion question to the group. Each student would take a turn by placing one **Talking Chip** into the middle of a table. Discussion continues until all students have used their chips. Rules for **Talking Chips** may vary depending on the activity. In some small-group settings, the first person to use a chip may not talk again until everyone else in the group has used a chip. However, in other cases the students may use their chips whenever they want during the dialogue, but once their chips are gone, they are unable to speak again until all other team members have used their chips. Once all the chips have been used, the students could pick up their chips and continue the process until the allotted time is up.

Tips and Variations

- **Clear Directions** and expectations should be set up regarding the use and management of this intervention. Consider allowing a few students to **Be the Model** in order to demonstrate the proper way to conduct the discussion.

75 Quick and Easy Solutions to Common Classroom Disruptions

TEACHER-APPROVED TOYS

Blurting Out in Whole Group | Side Talking | Rude/ Disrespectful Behavior | Zoning Out/ Lack of Focus | Doesn't Try/ Gives Up Easily

Overview

Some students find it difficult to keep their hands "focused" during class time. **Teacher-Approved Toys** are small items, such as a squishy ball, a slinky, or a stuffed animal, that students can use to occupy their hands.

Putting It All Together

When students are having difficulty keeping their hands to themselves or are using their hands in inappropriate ways, offer them **Teacher-Approved Toys.** These toys are pre-selected by the teacher to help the students occupy their hands in an appropriate manner. Before implementing this intervention, the teacher needs to help the student understand the use and function of the toy as well as the expectations and rules of use. The toy is used with the goal of increasing focus and on-task behavior, and it should not serve as a distraction to the student or to the other students in the class. The teacher should explain this intervention to the parents and even include them in the choice of item being used. **Teacher-Approved Toys** are beneficial in helping students keep their hands to themselves, stopping them from making inappropriate noises or gestures, and helping them focus for longer periods of time. The teacher should continue to monitor this strategy to ensure that the toy is being used appropriately, that the student is not bragging about the use of the toy to his or her peers, and that the toy is being effective in its intended use.

Tips and Variations

- Teachers should use **Clear Directions** when setting up this intervention with their students. Students should know where the toys should be placed when they are not in use, acceptable times at which they may use them, and what happens if they misuse the toys.

- A **Teacher-Approved Toy** can also be used as a **Concrete Reminder**.

TEACHING SPOT

Blurting Out in Whole Group | Side Talking | Rude/ Disrespectful Behavior | **Zoning Out/ Lack of Focus** | Doesn't Try/ Gives Up Easily

Overview

A **Teaching Spot** is a specific, consistently used location in the classroom that is utilized to gain students' attention for the purpose of focusing that attention on directions or key pieces of information. When the teacher reliably uses this intervention, students will learn to associate the spot in which the teacher stands with the need to focus their attention.

Putting It All Together

Although used during whole-group interactions, this intervention is particularly helpful for students who tend to easily lose focus. Instruct the students that when you stand in the identified spot, they will need to stop what they are doing, turn their bodies so they can see you, and listen to instructions or information. It is helpful to label the **Teaching Spot** with a poster, sign, or icon as a reminder. From that spot, the teacher then provides the important information, remembering to be brief and to focus on those pieces of information that are critical for students to know. Students will need to be trained in the procedures to follow when they are asked to focus their attention, including what to do when the teacher steps away from the **Teaching Spot**. Many teachers combine this intervention with an **Attention Signal**, **SLANT**, or **Engaging Frames**.

Tips and Variations

- For students who lose focus easily, remember to limit the amount of time they are being given verbal directions or information. Longwinded directions or lectures may actually reinforce unfocused behavior.

Overview

This intervention is simple yet powerful in that it helps to predispose the student to positive behavior by acknowledging cooperation and focus before it takes place.

Putting It All Together

Typically used at the beginning of a lesson or class period, **Thanks in Advance** is a brief, positive statement that recognizes a behavior that the teacher expects or wants to see from the student. Challenging students often expect to hear directives or warnings about what they shouldn't do or what they've done wrong in the past. For example, many students hear something like "Ethan, today we have a lot of work to do. You need to keep your mouth quiet today. I don't want to have to call home again." Those types of interactions can actually reinforce negative behavior because they highlight negative behavior. Instead, consider interacting with students in ways that highlight and show an expectation of positive behavior. For the example above, the teacher may say, "Ethan, we have a lot of work to do. I appreciate that you will work hard to be quiet during our work time. Thank you for putting in the effort to stay focused." **Thanks in Advance** statements should be made with a positive tone, a clear expectation of compliance, and no hint of sarcasm or doubt.

Tips and Variations

- This intervention is often used with **Be Brief, Be Positive, Be Gone; Greet and Read; Solicit Good Intentions**; or **Start Statements**.

- This intervention should not be used to negatively manipulate or guilt students into compliance. Rather, the purpose is to plant the seed of expected positive behavior.

THREE MORE MINUTES, AND . . .

| Blurting Out in Whole Group | Side Talking | Rude/ Disrespectful Behavior | Zoning Out/ Lack of Focus | Doesn't Try/ Gives Up Easily |

Overview

Some students who struggle to appropriately manage their time respond positively when the teacher offers short, specific time goals that provide them something desirable to work toward.

Putting It All Together

When a student is struggling to focus on a task or assignment, approach the student and inquire about his or her progress, ask questions, or gauge the factors that are preventing the student from focusing. If needed, provide clarification, re-direction, or encouragement, and follow up with a statement such as "Focus on this assignment for **Three More Minutes, and** then we can take a stretch break." A discrete, manageable task and a short time frame often provide students the incentive to refocus and complete the work. The time frame can be adjusted to meet the needs of the students, but it is important to remember that some children will just be further frustrated if given time frames that are too long or too short. For example, a child will not likely respond positively to hearing "Focus on this assignment for forty more minutes, and then you can take a stretch break." When using this intervention, ensure that whatever is offered after the time frame is desirable. If a child is asked to focus for a few more minutes on an undesirable task only to be given another undesirable task, this intervention will not be effective.

Tips and Variations

● Some students may need to be shown specifically how to focus on a task for the short term. In those cases, encourage them to **Chunk Tasks**.

● Consider combining this intervention with **Choice of Order**, **Color Codes**, or **Proximity**.

Overview

This intervention is an extension of the **Extend an Invitation** technique for giving challenging students a specific method to participate in whole-group classroom activities.

Putting It All Together

Many challenging students respond positively when they are given a very specific, concrete way to participate positively in classroom activities. Much as the **Planted Questions** intervention offers students the chance to think about their answers to specific questions, this intervention provides students with specific jobs to complete during the lesson. Before the lesson, speak privately with a student and request his or her assistance during an upcoming lesson. Explain that you'd like the student's help in keeping track of certain behaviors. For example, you may say, "I'd like your help in keeping track of how many questions I ask during the lesson. As your teacher, I am working on asking better, more in-depth questions. So, I want you to keep track of the number of times I ask questions that start with the word *why, when, how, which,* or *where*." After the lesson, ensure that the student shares the information with you, and consider having the student help to analyze the data or **Graph the Results**. This intervention serves to give the student a specific purpose, but it also models that the teacher is interested in continually learning and is committed to improving his or her teaching ability.

Tips and Variations

- Teacher or class characteristics that can be tracked include teacher wait time, questions asked of boys vs. girls, personal teacher quirks such as the use of *um* or hand motions, teacher movement around the room, or questions asked by students.

- As a caution, do not ask a student to track the behavior or misbehavior of other students in the class. This may set the student up in an adversarial position, and there is no guarantee that the information collected is accurate.

TRAFFIC LIGHT

| Blurting Out in Whole Group | Side Talking | Rude/ Disrespectful Behavior | Zoning Out/ Lack of Focus | Doesn't Try/ Gives Up Easily |

Overview

The **Traffic Light** is a tool that students can use to signal to their teachers when they need help.

Putting It All Together

There may be a few students in the classroom who need to be monitored more closely for appropriate behavior or for potential help during independent work time. For those students, provide a picture of a **Traffic Light** with a paperclip attached. A student places the paperclip on the color of the **Traffic Light** that indicates his or her need for assistance. This intervention allows the student to communicate in a nonverbal manner without having to publicly proclaim the need for help. For example, when a student places the paperclip on green, this indicates to the teacher that assistance is needed. The yellow indicates that a student is slowing down and needs the teacher to stop by to check, but is able to continue working. The red may indicate that the student is stuck and can't continue without immediate assistance from the teacher. The exact meanings of each color can be differentiated based on the needs of the students.

Tips and Variations

● This strategy may be combined with **Looks Like, Sounds Like, Feels Like**. The student(s) and teacher can talk about what red, yellow, and green will look like, sound like, and feel like when **Traffic Light** is being used effectively in the classroom.

● As an option, give the student Styrofoam or plastic stackable drink cups of different colors. Define what each color represents, and train the student to place the appropriate colored cup on the top of the stack.

2 X 10 METHOD

Blurting Out in Whole Group | Side Talking | **Rude/ Disrespectful Behavior** | Zoning Out/ Lack of Focus | Doesn't Try/ Gives Up Easily

Overview

The **2 x 10 Method** is a way to connect with students by taking 2 minutes a day for 10 consecutive days to engage a student in a personal conversation with the purpose of finding commonalities and deepening the relationship.

Putting It All Together

Establishing trusting, sincere relationships with challenging students is necessary in order for them to thrive in the classroom. This intervention helps to build teacher-student trust through the investment of time and effort on behalf of the teacher. It requires that the teacher invest at least 2 minutes per day for 10 days in a row with the purpose of finding out more about the student. During this time, the teacher desires to get to know the student's interests, ideas, thoughts, hobbies, and favorite things. Basically, the teacher takes the time to figure out what makes the student tick and to help figure out what is engaging and interesting to the student. During the 2 x 10 time, the teacher expresses genuine interest in the student as a person and learner, not just in his or her progress in a particular subject or grades in school. In fact, teachers should avoid stressing the importance of grades, behavior, and participation. Students will often see through that obvious attempt to manipulate. Instead, make the effort to develop the relationship and find specific things you appreciate and like about the student.

Tips and Variations

- The time allotments of 2 minutes and 10 days are just guidelines. The purpose is to invest time and effort getting to know the student better.

- Avoid any appearance of impropriety, and do this intervention during the school day with the full knowledge and support of the family and administration.

- It is not necessary that you do this intervention in private. Teachers often conduct the 2 x 10 discussions during passing times, at lunch, while taking students to the bus or parent pick-up area, or during the few minutes before school starts.

VICTORY LIST

Blurting Out in Whole Group · **Side Talking** · **Rude/ Disrespectful Behavior** · **Zoning Out/ Lack of Focus** · **Doesn't Try/ Gives Up Easily**

Overview

A **Victory List** is a record of successes, triumphs, and accomplishments that a student shares with an adult of his or her choosing.

Putting It All Together

Some students expect to have their negative behaviors constantly highlighted, pointed out, and made public. As a result, many of them come to see themselves in a negative light or take on the role of the "bad" kids. The **Victory List** intervention highlights the areas where a student has grown, met or exceeded expectations, and experienced success. Speak privately with the student and provide a **Checklist** or a sheet of paper and ask the student to write down areas in which he or she has been successful for the day or period. Explain that victories do not have to be big things and they don't have to be solely focused on learning, grades, or academics. Depending on the confidence level of the student, the teacher may need to prompt the student with ideas or actions to list. For example, for students who struggle to keep their bodies under control, the teacher could say, "Julie, I noticed that when the groups lined up to get materials, you let two students in front of you so they could get what they needed. That was very thoughtful, and I would list that as a victory." **Victory Lists** do not need to be lengthy or complicated. In fact, some students may experience only a few victories in a day. When the victories are listed, ask the students to share the list with an adult of their choosing. Ask them to brag a little about themselves and to be proud of their accomplishments. The students could choose to share the list with another teacher, a paraprofessional, a parent, or even the principal.

Tips and Variations

- This intervention can be combined with **Communicate with Home**, **Graph the Results**, **Increase Feedback**, or **Personal Goals**.

- Part of the power of this intervention is that it is shared with an adult of the student's choosing. However, ensure that the adult gives proper encouragement and doesn't show disappointment if the victories are not numerous or in the expected areas.

WHAT YOU COULD HAVE SAID WAS

Blurting Out in Whole Group | **Side Talking** | **Rude/ Disrespectful Behavior** | Zoning Out/ Lack of Focus | Doesn't Try/ Gives Up Easily

Overview

Contrary to popular belief, we don't learn from our mistakes. We learn from *processing*, *thinking about*, and *reflecting* on mistakes. Many teachers assume that a consequence alone will be enough to change behavior, but challenging students need the opportunity to reflect and think about their behavior in combination with suggestions and alternatives for future behavior.

Putting It All Together

It is important to note that in order to reflect on behavior, one must be in the proper mindset to think critically about what has happened. As a result, this intervention will be successful only if it is used when students are calm, open, and willing to listen. **What You Could Have Said Was** is typically done in a one-on-one or private setting where the student does not have to worry about peer approval. Debrief the student about an incident and offer suggestions about what could have been said or done as an alternative to what was actually said or done. For example, for a student who impulsively blurted out a rude comment to a peer, the teacher may say, "When you feel frustrated when the other students don't listen to you, what you could say is... ." However, this intervention could also be used to give feedback to a child who exhibited positive behavior during a difficult time. For example, the teacher could say, "I noticed when the other students teased you about your handwriting, you stayed calm. You could have gotten really mad and called them names but you didn't."

Tips and Variations

- Ensure that when you provide feedback, it is genuine and not given in a sarcastic tone. In addition, it is important to validate the student's emotions and experiences even when the student is difficult to deal with.

- This intervention is powerful because it requires students to reflect, and when used correctly, it also opens up a line of communication between the teacher and the student that is focused on problem solving rather than punishment alone.

Suggested Reading

Applestein, C. (1998). *No such thing as a bad kid*. Weston, MA: The Gifford School.

Boynton, M., & Boynton, C. (2005). *The educator's guide to preventing and solving discipline problems*. Alexandria, VA: Association for Supervision and Curriculum Development.

Breaux, A., & Whitaker, T. (2010). *50 ways to improve student behavior*. Larchmont, NY: Eye On Education.

Burke, K. (2008). *What to do with the kid who . . .* . Thousand Oaks, CA: Corwin Press.

Chapman, G., & Campbell, R. (1997). *The five love languages of children*. Chicago, IL: Northfield Publishing.

Chapman, C., & Vagle, N. (2011). *Motivating students: 25 strategies to light the fire of engagement*. Bloomington, IN: Solution Tree Press.

Charles, C. M. (2000). *The synergetic classroom: Joyful teaching and gentle discipline*. New York, NY: Longman Press.

Cummings, C. (2000). *Winning strategies for classroom management*. Alexandria, VA: Association for Supervision and Curriculum Development.

Curwin, R., Mendler, A., & Mendler, B. (2008). *Discipline with dignity: New challenges, new solutions*. Alexandria, VA: Association for Supervision and Curriculum Development.

DePorter, B., Reardon, M., & Singer-Nourie, S. (1998). *Quantum teaching: Orchestrating student success*. New York, NY: Allyn and Bacon.

Dweck, C. (2008). *Mindset: The new psychology of success*. New York, NY: Ballantine Books.

Edwards, J. (2010). *Inviting students to learn: 100 tips for talking effectively with your students*. Alexandria, VA: Association for Supervision and Curriculum Development.

Goldstein, N., Martin, S., & Cialdini, R. (2008). *Yes!: 50 scientifically proven ways to be persuasive*. New York, NY: Free Press.

Harris, B. (2010). *Battling boredom: 99 strategies to spark student engagement*. Larchmont, NY: Eye On Education.

Jackson, R. (2011). *How to motivate reluctant learners*. Alexandria, VA: Association for Supervision and Curriculum Development.

Koenig, L. (2007). *Smart discipline for the classroom*. Thousand Oaks, CA: Corwin Press.

Kottler, J. (2008). *Students who drive you crazy*. Thousand Oaks, CA: Corwin Press.

Lavoie, R. (2007). *The motivation breakthrough: 6 secrets to turning on the tuned-out child*. New York, NY: Touchstone.

McCarney, S. (2006). *The pre-referral intervention manual*. Columbia, MO: Hawthorne Educational Services.

Mendler, A. (2001). *Connecting with students*. Alexandria, VA: Association for Supervision and Curriculum Development.

Mendler, A. (1997). *Power Struggles: Successful techniques for educators*. Rochester, NY: Discipline Associates.

Sullo, B. (2009). *The motivated student: Unlocking the enthusiasm for learning*. Alexandria, VA: Association for Supervision and Curriculum Development.

Tileston, D. (2004). *What every teacher should know about classroom management and discipline*. Thousand Oaks, CA: Corwin Press.

Waller, R. (2008). *The educator's guide to solving common behavior problems*. Thousand Oaks, CA: Corwin Press.

Index of Interventions by Behavior

For students who **Side Talk**	For students who are **Rude or Disrespectful**
Audio Recording, 5	Apologize, 3
Be the Model, 7	Audio Recording, 5
Behavior Tracking, 10	Be Brief, Be Positive, Be Gone, 6
Concrete Reminders, 20	Behavior Contracts, 9
Eye Contact, 27	Choice of Order, 13
Headphones, 34	Course Evaluation, 21
I Messages, 36	Extend an Invitation, 26
If-Then Statements, 37	Eye Contact, 27
Learn to Ignore, 39	5-Minute Focus Group, 28
Photographic Evidence, 45	Give a Gift, 30
Private Office, 48	Give a Job, 31
Proximity, 49	I Messages, 36
Secret Signal, 54	If-Then Statements, 37
Solicit Good Intentions, 58	Learn to Ignore, 39
Sponge Activities, 61	Minimize Anxiety, 42
Start Strong, End Strong, 64	Offer the Door, 43
Talking Chips, 66	Personal Goals, 44
Thanks in Advance, 69	Positive Self-Talk, 47
What You Could Have Said Was, 75	Ramp Up Relevance, 51
	Right to Pass, 53
	Solicit Good Intentions, 58
	Sponge Activities, 61
	Start Strong, End Strong, 64
	Teacher-Approved Toys, 67
	Thanks in Advance, 69
	Three More Minutes, and . . ., 70
	Track the Lesson, 71
	2 x 10 Method, 73
	What You Could Have Said Was, 75

For students who **Zone Out or Lack Focus**	For students who **Don't Try or Give Up Easily**
A Head Start, 1	A Head Start, 1
Advance Organizers, 2	Advance Organizers, 2
Be Brief, Be Positive, Be Gone, 6	Be Brief, Be Positive, Be Gone, 6
Bean Bag, 8	Bean Bag, 8
Check-In Statements, 11	Behavior Contracts, 9
Checklists, 12	Check-In Statements, 11
Choice of Order, 13	Checklists, 12
Chunk Tasks, 14	Chunk Tasks, 14
Color Codes, 17	Closed Fist, 16
Eliminate Distractions, 23	Course Evaluation, 21
Engaging Frames, 25	Engaging Frames, 25
Extend an Invitation, 26	Extend an Invitation, 26
5-Minute Focus Group, 28	5-Minute Focus Group, 28
Headphones, 34	Focus on Process, 29
Planted Questions, 46	Give a Gift, 30
Private Office, 48	Minimize Anxiety, 42
Proximity, 49	Personal Goals, 44
Ramp Up Relevance, 51	Planted Questions, 46
Sentence Starters, 55	Positive Self-Talk, 47
Special Seating, 59	Proximity, 49
Stand and Stretch, 62	Ramp Up Relevance, 51
Teacher-Approved Toys, 67	Right to Pass, 53
Teaching Spot, 68	Sentence Starters, 55
Three More Minutes, and…, 70	Stand and Stretch, 62
Traffic Light, 72	Stories, 65
	Three More Minutes, and…, 70
	Track the Lesson, 71
	Traffic Light, 72

Bryan Harris and Cassandra Goldberg

— Notes —

— Notes —